D0331921

SIGNAGE

Copyright ©1987 by Alan Davies.

This book was made possible, in part, by grants from
the National Endowment for the Arts and the New York
State Council on the Arts.

ISBN: 0-937804-24-X
Library of Congress Catalog Card Number: 87-60108

Cover art by Richard Prince.

Production by Susan Bee and Nightwood Editions.

ROOF BOOKS
are published by
The Segue Foundation
300 Bowery
New York, N.Y. 10012

SIGNAGE

Alan Davies

ROOF

CONTENTS

PURSUE VERITABLE SIMPLES

One. The functions of criticism.

There are too many reasons to write criticism, be it critical (discursive/excisive) essaying or, critical (excisive/discursive) book reviewing. Too many reasons surround the writing itself.

This latter enunciates itself twice: "the writing itself$_1$" or the mode of critical approach, "the writing itself$_2$" or that which is approached. And here the assignation of number assigns the grammar: either could have preceded. And, again and, in fact, the writing itself is that which does.

The functions of criticism, and particularly of book reviews, are infatuated with, and activated by, a past. Criticism sells the book ("pushing the book"), it sells criticism, it sells two authors. Perhaps it has in instances begun to approach the present, provided a present not too critical of the past.

Criticism "advances" the reader, effecting (affecting?) a change in understanding, of style perhaps. Perhaps this constitutes a diversion, a sub-category, of the critic's intention to understand the considered writing. These approachings may magnify themselves, they may aim, indirectly, to change an or the entire social matrix: (but this is algebra).

Criticism intransitively records a history. Intransitively because, taking history as an object/function it is equally taken by history as a function/object. Criticism makes of itself an expression of history as/through literature. Being written it is a second history. Being writing it is being historicization.

These, then, vertical aspects of criticism: its cutting through time; its cutting, through time.

Criticism has a lateral aspect, which it shares with its objects and which it derives from its methods: to write excellently.

Two. Criticism's approach.

Criticism approaches. In this it implies its aggressive/submissive trait.

Criticism is tautologically aggressive: criticism pursues criticism. This aggressive pursuit produces its stature, a production which will not because it can not separate it from writing.

Criticism is empirically (historically) submissive: it pursues an object.* It takes an object as subject, it subjects an object. So-called "secondary writing."

The aggressive functions, strongly considered, are submissive. Criticism pursues. However vaguely uncertain of its object, it flees. Equally: take an object: aggress: and excellently and deservedly so, when it takes that object without discernment of its sameness/difference.**

Criticism accepts itself without judgement, having judged (accepted) itself into the position from which to do so.

Three. The materials of critical examination.

The materials of critical examination hold their history. The materials of critical examination have their present; "to have" is the verb unavoidably and always conjugating itself in the past. No one will "have" the writing in the future. The materials of critical examination have their future: in this way, they begin to anticipate and fabricate critical writings as object.

This divided view falls into itself in the middle. The materials of critical examination have their present. The materials of critical examination have their tools. The materials write

---

* It may avoid this in taking one without (having) pursuing it. The past, then, has been placed within its attendant brackets.
** A ratio whose sum is always zero.

themselves, they won't be separate from writing, such that their writing of them is not permitted separateness, or exclusion. The critical writing is writing writing, because the writing explains it.

Criticism is the activity of non-distance, separating from the critic the activities of distance. The past and future materials are peculiar fetishes: they are constantly sold as such. And it is a very great distance, to non-distance.

The materials of criticism are, then, the tools which, as itself, the object-text is offering. Within this most critical of presents, no tools are re-sold in the critical exemption criticism makes for its text. The materials are their tools and the tools their own exemplary potential.

Four. Criticism at its best at the present time.

When the object is approached directly there is therefore no object. There is no condescension, and the object is not declined. Criticism writes directly across to the text/object such that this "across" goes into the object; the distance is abolished, not the directness.

The reader of criticism looks in two directions, realizes self as the pierced object (substance) of each, as one. The triangle (text/reader/criticism(2nd reader)) is flattened: the line. This makes for the reader of critical writing the exercise of not having the obvious and the assigned place. The reader works at each, him and her self.

The book begins to be gone as the object of criticism. Criticism achieves its status as object, and knows the difficult limits of status; the object with an object: the schizophrenic. The reader who questions the difference, the sameness, of the two objects, the text and the critical text, becomes the critical being in both, the one in the one. It is learned that there is one. The critic, making of critical text an object, looses equal objects together into the world.

Criticism achieves text status, not abnegating the word "original," the word "originary," to its object-text; nor any longer taking for itself a secondary safety. To the advantage of

both, criticism is strong enough to be consumed as itself:
(Problem: the avoidance of non-fetish status). But at least the
"original text," the "critical object," is not any longer spoken
at (Problem: if criticism escapes, by easy routes, the definition
implicit in its name, the original text escapes notice).

But and against these problems, criticism participates with
the object/text. The problem here is that the reader escapes
notice, recognizing this their absence as the difficulty of reading
("both"). Perhaps, and this difficulty can be, the readers' own
reading of their potential, their excellence.

Criticism abandons its book-selling function without
abandoning the book; with its interest in its materials, precisely,
the book, and itself, it promotes to the reader those tools
which, if it has been worth the attention, always an indulgence,
the book has already best promoted itself. Criticism reiterates
but recognizes in reiteration only a lowest acceptable common
denominator of reading experience.

The criticism is an agent the original texts appear to
demand in their imagined efforts to make the reader write.
Criticism is an accomplice of those things which make it pos-
sible to live; it accomplishes them.

LIES

Truth is lies that have hardened.

This should be obvious from the fact that the obverse is also correct. The same obviousness obtains for correctness.

Truth, which will never be more than the notion of truth, keeps for itself only its own over-guarded presences. It is the equator without hemispheres, without a globe. This line, which merely appears to establish itself, is non-equatorial, in extremis.

Truth is the purest notions of dominations, not without persons, not without social exigencies, and not aside from the facets of the experienced tracts of truth. It is, in and by itself, the misnomer.

It is most certainly not true, not not true. It is the failed tautology, tautology without equatability, the terms of which are so very easily subsumed by the notions of there being terms.

Truth is the effort of intention to make of space protracted space, of time, protracted time.

The distance between truth and that which is known is that distance between intention and that which is truth. Truth is the shifter among concrete fact, the tightest of attentive experience, and the most indissoluble of intents.

Truth succumbs to a pressure of indifference. This makes of

"it" "truth."

Hard words don't get called true, except on the verges of hatred. This is a failure which specializes, and in itself, but the most solid things know this and it is they whereby we know that we have been otherwise mistaken.

Truth articulates itself only in relations with non-truths. Facts don't make these mistakes, because they stand in, for, in for, and as, some kind of solidity.

Truth articulates, it mentions, itself, only in relation with things which are not true, not because opposites are necessary (they are not), but because truth is a special form of the untrue and thereby finds itself most articulate in that presence.

The realm of truth is the realm of the alphabet. Thus is recognized its limitation: that truth is completely inscribed within the alphabet.

Truth is that flourish which a mind makes in an effort to make of itself a perfection, an aura which it will not mount without the angles of straight arts.

Truth.
I.e.
The idea of truth.

If you walk down the street as truth you walk down the street the other side of the street from violence.

Truth is some thing which resembles, as its exterior, some other thing. It is the appearance of the exterior of this thing, and without it, as evidence, which makes of its semblance, a thing wherein we recognize a truth.

The practice of truth is a hollowing of what is real, the removal of the substance to ensure the (false) sanctity, the (false) perpetuity, of the form.

Form is, as such, deserving of those interests which thus elevate it. Truth, in its methods, merely imitates the just formulations of form, and within the results of those methods which it must then attempt to erect, to stabilize, as facts. Their appearance as supreme facts is merely a function of their resemblance, which they have, after all, manufactured, to forms. It is perhaps only the extreme effort which must be made to make a statement appear true, which makes us call it a truth when we recognize it. Truth is the evaluation of the boundaries to which it reaches, its limits, its husk. That is to say, when we say of something that it is true, we say that it has stopped.

Each moment is a retrograde moment, and it is moments which are productive of truth.

Truth is present only to itself, which is why nobody notices it until it is talked about, and why everyone notices it when it is.

Truth and lies. That is not the question.

The Indeterminate Interval: From History to Blur

(Coauthor: Nick Piombino)

Event-related signals can reveal subtle differences in mental processes. The wave that appears when the mind confronts nonsense is easily distinguished from the one that results from simple surprise, according to Dr. Steven A. Hillyard of the University of California at San Diego, even though there is surprise in encountering a word that transforms a reasonable sentence into nonsense. He and Dr. Marta Kutas reported discovery of the coping-with-nonsense signal recently in the journal *Science*. This signal appears about 400 milliseconds (four-tenths of a second) after the event that causes it and appears on a graph as a negative voltage. It is called the N400 wave. The brain's signature for surprise is found in another wave called P300, a positive voltage appearing 300 milliseconds after its event.

The newly discovered signal seems to appear in response to a nonsense statement, even in prolonged testing, Dr. Hillyard said. Even after encountering many sentences that degenerate into nonsense, the brain evidently cannot stop trying to make sense of them. The special response to nonsense does not appear if a word is simply misspelled, but only if it is a legitimate word used in a nonsense way.

'This N400 wave seems to be tapping into a higher mental process than any that we've been studying with ERP's during the past 10 years,' said Dr. Hillyard. 'It depends on a person having a sophisticated language ability.'   *The New York Times*, March 11, 1980.

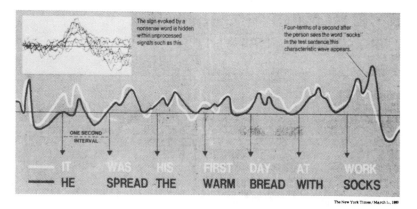

The sign evoked by a nonsense word is hidden within unprocessed signals such as this.

Four-tenths of a second after the person sees the word "socks" in the test sentence this characteristic wave appears.

ONE SECOND INTERVAL

IT   WAS   HIS   FIRST   DAY   AT   WORK

HE   SPREAD THE   WARM   BREAD   WITH   SOCKS

The New York Times/March 11, 1980

It wasn't until 45 years later that Heisenberg stated in a new theory of physics what Mallarmé knew in 1880: 'A Dice Throw Will Never Abolish Chance.' Heisenberg demonstrated that you cannot measure a particle's speed and its location at the same time; out of these factors evolved a theory of indeterminacy, a theory of constant uncertainty.

> Stochastic: (Greek, *stochazein*, to shoot with a bow at a target; that is, to scatter events in a partially random manner, some of which achieve a preferred outcome.) If a sequence of events combines a random component with a selective process so that only certain outcomes of the random are allowed to endure, that sequence is said to be *stochastic*.
> Gregory Bateson, *Mind and Nature* (1979, p. 230).

The Freudian theory of free association inscribes a stochastic situation: the analyst asks the analysand to speak every thought entering his/her mind, the analyst sifts those thoughts through the analyst's mind, at some point stops the flow, selectively. Free associations, the random component; the analyst's interpreting intervention, the selective.

One interprets, with fairly great certainty, a probable outcome; the position of the individual units is relatively unknown. The relationship between writing and reading also describes a line of uncertainty. Publishing locates, within a historical moment, the position of a thought.

In metric reading (i.e. reading at a certain momentum) the reader reads the momentum; in contrast, within the Mallarméan idea, one reads the space as a schematic which resonates between two sets of intervalic waves: one, the originating creative energy which generated the poem, and two, the vibrations of the mind in the presence of the poem. In prose, the language locale is not determined; within the poem's determinations, momentum is very clear. What is actually read is scattered throughout the moment-by-moment information; the reading is continuously a prosodic furtherance of the text.

The use of associative rather than fixed descriptive language keeps open the experience which is the original and repeated referent. If momentum were substituted for place, a symbol, a representation, certain details of the experience would be left open which would be forgotten if fixed in precise and linguistic terms.

Free association — 'evenly suspended attention' — is precise, working a wider field. The Mallarméan layout of words allows for a wider field of concentration. The specific words of prose are not determined by spacing. Satie's furniture music, though simple and delicate, permits the mind to take it(self) an enormous quantity of places. Each Satie note is a pointer in a possible direction, a precise and enjoyable structure of attention. Volume of attention is not insisted upon by the music, but is permitted.

Duchamp: 'object' language, 'language' objects. A thing associated to its idea: an equation between the object and the language about the object. Surrounding objects remind us at all times of symbolic movements within. In the presence of objects, the two are never completely divergent from each other.

1900: the seeming enigmatic (the mysterious) as a different way of getting inclusiveness, with the precision of all-inclusiveness. Over-focusing on the fixing of the historical particular, in memory, misses the field productive of the original particular and cuts off evolution of new particulars which might have come from the original field. A particular thing is the model, the example, the convincing thing within what is said. Around 1900 people began to realize the historical view to be a distortion: leave the focusing to the reader. Both, measure the specifics and, grasp the sensations and experiences behind the laying-down of those particulars, to invoke the original experience, the originating state of mind. It is the difference between an exhaustive list of particulars and a schematic performing a number of exhaustive lists of particulars (which permits to anyone their filling-in). The power of persuasion, the power of giving the experience does not come from the photographic, the documentary, the 'accounting.'

*

Memory becomes the place, the locus, relative to which particulars get filed (both senses). Filing a thing whittles it, by putting it in that one place. Fitting in, placing things between, relates to the idea of interval. Fragmenting produces interval. The interval has a place, fits into a larger whole, a larger continuum. But it is still a very specific moment, productive of an instance of pulse, a measure, like sonar, a metronome. Intervals pulse, inscribing the certain amount of distance that has been gone through.

In Duchamp's 'Network of Stoppages' (1914), the measure is inscribed as part of the structure; the structure is presented as an instance of mental measurement.

Periods (and in the grammatical sense) of history: the envisioning that *that* would exist makes it happen, the consciousness of periods makes history. Uncertainty and doubt create much more truth in the renderings and findings; 'this is it,' the schematics, the suggestive things, the connectives... by the time it is fixed it is changed. The act of fixing is time-consuming, time-altering, time-debilitating; it shifts what time means, stops the flow (this constitutes the argument with history). A grasped history is lost when the concern is to keep track of it in a precise way. Without the ability to measure place and momentum equally and at once, nothing really happened. Intervals are not confusing, they are allowable of confusion, in not distorting chaos.

The Egyptians personified in their pyramid building the type of consciousness that wants to totally expand the scale of human time in the universe versus the actuality of that chronology. The time becomes something in which human terms of death and life are altered dramatically by the externalization of scale.

*

Time is investigated in investigating the possibilities of the interval (Mallarmé, Debussy, Ravel, Satie); the experimentation determines what can happen within a certain interval, without spoiling the composition of the whole: the point is made in a moment. The work assumes attentiveness without demanding it; the work values the other, trusts its reader. The work distributes not points but the process of distribution; the reader also distributes the activity.

Mallarmé's mysteries, ellipses, vectors that aren't followed through or that establish themselves suddenly and curiously in a place where they had not been expected, value the activity of their reception unrestrictedly. Williams' statement 'No ideas but in things' is rigid, minisculing, a limit, a sort of advertising slogan. Persons exist in the midst of ideas, even choosing to represent ideas. Interval gives an impression of scope, the absolute size of the idea, rather than an assertive focusing on the self-importance of the particular. Because thought is experienced in intervals it is possible to move from the somewhat willed and somewhat random places that are reached in thinking, volumes of distance in space and time.

   Around 1900 the mapping began of the variable distances with possible volumes of thought, to note the volume implicit in those distances which constitute it. The particles are wonderfully multifarious but they change; the distances, the relationships, obtain for new particles, new particulars.

*

The lines composed of shorter and longer lines are the threads.
The places where they meet are the stitches.
Language is the needle.
Thought is the thread.
The cloth is experience.
The places where the stitches meet are memory, are history.

> interval: 1. a space between things: a void space intervening between any two objects; as an *interval* between two houses or walls. 2. a period of time between any two points or events, or between the return of like conditions; as, the *interval* between two wars; an *interval* in fever. 3. in music, the difference in pitch between two tones. 4. the extent of difference between two qualities, conditions, etc.

Art that doesn't push to where it has to go, that is more intervalic, admits of indeterminacy. (Morse code/computers). It is a function of attention (see *A Note Upon the Mystic Writing Pad*, Freud, 1925). The way attention was looked at, what attention had to be for things to be discovered, for attention to be attention, shifted around 1880 to 1905. For attention to be discontinuous was no longer for it to be an attention that wasn't rigorous; taken into account was what attention is, the way the mind works. In studying people with neurotic minds, Freud studied what was fragmented, he studied intervals. Neuroses are intervals, static on the line. Static becomes a part of the music; in that random component, for that part of the stochastic thought, enters the new thing, the other, from the other thing; from the other person, from the object, from the other person, from the other the other thing. The other music must be unidirectional, not bi-polar.

At the sub-atomic level, almost existence, or forever existence, or other existence, is as much a part of the regular flow as is the 'regular flow' itself. What almost happened, happened. There is an art which includes this blur, demanding focus: the level where the virtual, or the about-to-be, or what came before, or what almost existed but without extension, is as much a part of measurable reality, of experience. Choice breaks the flow, must be part of the music, is part of thought.

We know discrete things before knowing their names as objects. The object state is the blur between the thing and the word: the beginning to perceive that a word is getting attached to a thing, the photon-like almost-being of either, is as much a part of the world as the thing and the word and later the fact. The mind also sees the names as having discreet qualities before knowing what the word represents. The word itself is at first a thing, then becoming an object representing an object. The words are early seen as also a world of objects. The turning of meaningful sounds into words parallels the turning of thing into object. As each process progresses, words attach to objects increasingly. The process never ends; learning a thing and a name of a thing rehappens in every single interval. The name of the object is not on hold. One reexperiences less as time goes on, as experience becomes less new; one continues to notice it first as a thing, then as an object. In calling into meaning phrases or words or language that is read, the process of focussing from the original conception of what was meant into, e.g., a conception of what the author means or, e.g., what is assigned as the personal meaning, is the continuous process of the intervalic. Intervals are moments off-rhythm between the identification, interspersed into the identification, happen as often, are as much a part of it as the 'it' is which is the goal. Art admits the blur towards which it was called into being. Keep it in moving, blurred-action, sense. Static: no static.

Some of the focussing is seen in the creation of the text (im-parting an appearance of ambiguity, but) actually holding in the ambiguity that it moved from in trying to eliminate the blur existing before the final thing was there. The blur is a bath into which the writer-reader relationship constantly dips itself; the bath consists in the movement in consciousness from thing to object-representation, from meaningful sound to word, from morpheme to phoneme. Those movements are mimed in the writing-reading process, an immersion in the development of a consciousness: the mind of the modes of writer and reader. Stein: that genius is reading and writing equally. The inter-active process mimes experience more convincingly than a writer's giving of a script; rather than which, the intervals extant at the moment of creation, the original blur. The work is a moebius strip, a three-dimensional figure of the infinity of this process. The slight unravelling is experience, the further unravelling is codification; in more unravelling *when* codifying, remember the original unravelling more ragged than the unrav-elling thing of the present, capture more of the essential original unraggedness. It wouldn't be a moebius strip because there are no continuous lines.

> The uncertainty principle reveals that as we penetrate deeper and deeper into the subatomic realm, we reach a certain point at which one part or another of our picture of nature becomes blurred, and there is no way to reclarify that part without blurring another part of the picture! It is as though we are adjusting a moving picture that is slightly out of focus. As we make the final adjustments, we are astonished to discover that when the right side of the picture clears the left side of the picture becomes completely unfocused and nothing in it is recog-nizable. When we try to focus the left side of the picture, the right side starts to blur and soon the situation is reversed. If we try to strike a balance between these two extremes, both sides of the picture return to a recognizable condition, but in no way can we remove the original fuzziness from them.
>
> Gary Zukov, *The Dancing Wu Li Masters* (1979, p. 111).

*

Looking for the locus of something, defining its place, fixing it, also fixes an actual instance of time. The locus is a specific place which fixes; fixing on a perspective finds a moment in history and thus the unit of language in which it occurred.

Association occurs on the grid of experience: one pull is

towards place which leads towards time; the other pull on specific association is towards its meaning, the generalization that comes out of its meaning, and its structure. An association tied to a place or a mapping grows out of a pull against its meaning, generalization, and structure. Where and when a thing took place grows out of familiarization, a part of learning; generalization, the other part. The direction towards acquiring facts and knowledge and learning, through familiarization, builds up a kind of transference to that style which is what is meant by the ego. The memory function of familiarization is historicity; the other direction of the association is towards its meaning, its generalization, and the actual structural part of the mind of that association. Each pull is a relief from the other's pressure and at the same time a stress on the particular association.

An epoch in the life of a thought can be likened to an accent mark over a vowel, which is also a place mark; it indicates a certain kind of place, a certain emphasis (the lines on a topological map, grammatical oversimplification of that actual fact of height above sea level). Accenting occurs in the same kind of locus as topological marking; the plotting of everyone's enunciation of an acute mark over the vowel *e* at the end of a verb would produce something approximating that thing which says 150' above sea level.

Say place, names. Names place, place place, names names; place locus. Saying 'here's the spot' names it, locates it, defines it; it *also* establishes the who of saying it, not what is said. It is a total temporal statement. 'This is Kansas but, *not anymore!* Now it's some totally other place. We're still calling it Kansas for the sake of convenience, but it ain't *Kansas* no more.'

*

There's a place that you're going from and a place that you're going to; to get to that place, that tracking, is as worthwhile as the endpoint of going, because while you're going there you find other things and those things are related to the final place; that helps to define what it is when you get there. New combinations and connections are experienced. In finding your locus you redefine it again each time, systematically finding new coordinates. When you try to solve the meaning of a work and you examine it looking for that spot, this tracking is what the composition is. You make a new grid to get there but that new grid is today's grid, a new place; giving you a new coordinate vs the one you're looking for, a new name, a new meaning. It's alway constantly destructible, or deconstructible. If you view the bride of language as the seductress or seductor of language then you view it as the reader and the writer at the same time. Which posits them in the same place at the same time, the text not so much a map as a median for that unity of place. Does the train for Brighton come at 2:02 or is 2:02 the time when the train for Brighton comes? The reader and the writer are in one place, as a seductor or seductress of language; finding each other, *being* each other, being both, being *one*, being language. On the way to seducing the bride of language, differing types of separateness exist, and then a unity, then a new separateness, a new unity. (It's at that point that confusion about publishing arises, raising the questions of which road one is on relative to production.)

*

Field reading involves thinking about place in relation to meaning. Field reading relates to a reading of musical notes, to connecting the dots, to the gestalt reading; the mind takes certain evidence, accounts for it. The mind takes the place of dot factors (whether they can be put in an index, in a codifying system) which are themselves a field which the mind uses to connect them; it is already assumed in the thing that is happening that the individual moments are not historicized because one needn't later know their precise position, the position is only needed immediately, for the time being, in order to get to the more general picture. Nonetheless, the dots do have a place; one could historicize around that particular place and build back up from the original impression. In field reading one has both: you can fix it, or you can de-fix it later: you can fix it when reading or experiencing it but you can also de-assemble the original impulses because the original fixing remains. The individual elements are given as a field in which they can be perceived separately or in which the field can be perceived as a given, as a piece of evidence, a fact. Field reading involves the factualization by the reader of the given particulars. The reader doesn't need to remember what was just read but can also remember it in its given position.

The originating positioning is itself approximate, but going back to a specific particular or grouping of particulars, the original relations are still maintained. It is a matter of scale. A particular grouping in a text permits the reader to retrace the meaning of the originating moment through the positioning. Giving the reader this field experience provides the possibility of the mind's, e.g., expansion of any grouping. To permit this reading the writer eliminates the historicization implied by the impression that the particular graphemic points are historical; their momentousness depends alone on the fact that their position communicates.

Dada reverses historicity: the historicity becomes the meddling whimsical random element that is consciously introduced into the flow of the interval, in a reversing of ego. Dada doesn't substantiate history; instead it presents an experience of specific random moments being what they are, still with specificity and still with the randomization. Duchamp reestablishes as one perception the seen field and the meaning within the mind, the multiple levels which constantly pulsate and fluctuate between the two, allowing for a multiplicity of connections; a trace of specific groupings remains within that multiplicity, the shape that happened at that particular moment in history. Dada reverses the historical within chance, the random component, the indeterminate. The modern notion that one has so much to do with what one imagines as having happened at a given moment is very much a part of Dada. Dada also saw chance as an element of history, laughed at it recognitively, saw the problems of too much historicism coming from any one direction.

That which takes into account the aspect of the ludicrous allows for a distancing from the subject material which makes it easier to experience. A writing unwilling to become ludicrous is unwilling to deal with its own specificity in time. The ludicrous permits relief from the awareness that a historical moment is the only time which permits its knowledge. If the gravity of the moment outweighs the accessibility of the knowledge, that is the pathetic.

Field reading looks for hidden connections in two otherwise irreconcilable areas, often with ludicrous results. A field reader makes the greatest possible use of any absurd connection between the particulars, making unforeseen connections out of the apparently ludicrous. There is always something to retrace.

There is an element of the mind which reshuffles the signals it experiences, reads them in different orders. Dreams and a lot of art perform this function, a function already built into and part of the blueprint of perception. In making an art that attempts to provide for a field reading experience, one opens up to direct apperception the experience of that part of the mind which screens experience. Field reading allows for the normal capacity of the mind to reshuffle experience, to see new connections than those which were thought when the mind originally formed the connections; field reading permits the mind to portray and perceive the actuality of reality as experienced.

> distortion in the process of focusing is focused on minutely so that the distortions themselves are the primary focus forcing the singular point (the sign) to intersect the matrix of time/experience

The constellation that forms the original patterns of what the reader tries to retrace: any point in the text permits the other points. The splicing of two parts refocuses them in a different way; focusing a small detail which may seem a flaw or snag in the whole fabric, discovers the points of tension, the points of most resistance. The mind, in its barest function, takes in the facts, sifts them, determining both its own daily need of facts and what it must do next; it finds those things which have the most gravity. The mind grows and links to other things when the unexpected things are linked; it scans elements, processes them and in doing so, reshuffles them for another something which the mind will invent. The mind evolves a blueprint out of what is already there, doesn't recognize where to go next, then explores and enumerates the possibilities, a part of the mind insisting on making the ludicrous connection. The odd connection permits a reexperience of what was originally recorded but not really experienced. The mind (language) reshuffles its fragments in order to attain the original hierarchy; reassembling it permits reprocessing from the new perspective.

Language in its structure is the transitional element that is held between persons; it can't be dismissed. In holding language commonly, persons build up a protective and necessary conventional code, as in all law, to try to equalize and stabilize and make as respectable or negotiable a currency as possible. There is understandably among human beings an enormous hesitancy to allow for aspects of language that have been held in check, to change the code of survival.

notes for <u>CONSTRUCTION</u>

Poems have to be constructed architecturally. That is, clusters of words and pieces of the poem must work to support other sections. This inter-supportive relationship should produce an architectonic effect. This is like the structuring that supports good music. It doesn't have to be obvious to work.

*

Any kind of repetition — alliteration, rhyme, repeated phrases — bind the poem together. Obvious repetitions (rhyme, refrain, etc.) have for the most part been used too much. But repetition of syntactical constructions, or of subtle combinations of sound, can make the poem. Refrains, inserted into the flow of the poem, can separate sections and slow down the movement.

*

Prosody is usually taught as rhyme, assonance, consonance, alliteration, rhythm, metre. But these only represent kinds of repetition that have been often used. The most useful aspects of construction aren't as easy to discuss, because they don't repeat as frequently and obviously. The relationship between each word and those that surround it, is what the poem is. But these relationships are more unique, harder to categorize.

*

Giorno's poems are built on mirror repetition of every phrase. This binds strands of the poem together like bonds of RNA DNA. This illustrates very strongly the possibility of architectural stress and support.

*

Punctuation separates pieces of syntax. Develop a feel for the relative distances imposed by different kinds of punctuation. The feeling for the different amounts of separation created by kinds of punctuation has to be developed by use, and its meaning and effect exist in that use. Punctuation is the hinge between phrases, clauses, etc.; it determines the distance between them, the pause, the silence.

*

In any small group of words, such as a stanza or verse paragraph, the punctuation is especially important. It provides one visual aspect that runs through the cluster of words. It helps define the looseness of the structure, giving it some amount of vegetative density. It holds pieces of the poem in relation to each other, and shows how each part grows away from and into the whole.

*

Let the reader decide whether it is prose or poetry; they will anyway. This newness, this uncertainty, will infuse the work with more vigor. Simply that more will be happening, the reader will be doing more.

*

The major things in prose are the stops and starts and the pauses. In poetry perhaps the pauses.

*

If you try something, use it. Your use of it will make it work.

*

It's obvious that more can be done with space and punctuation and volume in writing. I want to see how.

*

If there is music you like it can be absorbed and put in your poetry. Lyrics might run in your mind but your words will be more complex; and tunes, movements, structures will probably be obvious only to you.

*

Punctuation is pacing. It resembles such natural activities as

breathing, walking, fucking, it should also resemble the distri-
bution of objects in nature and around people.

*

If something makes an impression on your mind, use it in your
writing. What else could be important?

*

All of your writing — diary writing, criticism, ... — should be
equally interesting to you. This will insure an evenness of
attention and an even quality. It will keep you interested and
draw all aspects of your work together; greater intensity.

*

Your writing should be as varied as circumstance.

*

Poems should be polychromatic. They should emit in various
directions a variety of feelings, statements, sounds. The flow
of the poem will hold this variety toward some finish. The
aspects will be thrown off at each point by any of the devices
of the poem.

*

The "should" in these statements is no kind of imperative.
Like all criticism they best reflect only my own wishes for
my poems.

*

Poems should correspond substantially to the world the writer
lives in, and the world that lives in him or her. This corre-
spondence is the only essential accuracy. It gives the poem
its life.

*

At least occasionally, push for as much sound as possible and
still allow/maintain sense.

*

You could write continuously, trying to keep up. You'd run out
but then things would change, you'd put that down. As you
became more aware, you'd notice more of the changes that
occur, write them down, that down, trying to keep up, faster

until you could not write or type as fast. So how do you make the decision to write any thing.

Overwhelmed in a sense by the volume. That is the volume we divide and use, if we do.

*

When you use paragraphs or stanzas, you float groups of words on the page. Try to do this with variety. The various effects of direction and movement, density, relative volumes, contrasting or similar clusters, and so on, will create useful impressions.

*

Use forms of expression and syntax current to your culture experience. Provide evidence you understand how people around you are speaking. Speak with them.

*

For intensity, combine adjectives with nouns in ways not usual, or adverbs with verbs. Combining abstract nouns with concrete modifiers, or with other abstract terms, creates vibrant fluidity. Strings of strong words without weak connectives fill the poem with force (you can learn this from Ginsberg) like Chinese ideograms.

*

Develop an ability to not push words in usual channels. Hold words in your mind. They locate other words, appear next to them, among them. Hold unusual combinations; they hold unusual emotion information.

*

A poem isn't a product, final. It is itself productive of feeling, perhaps change.

*

Writing is a biological production. It proceeds between metabolism and self-perpetuation. It unites them, fuses them. It is organic, physical. The writer sets down on the page the gray white substance. It is generative. The page is like pollen; a reader picks it up.

*

If you feel compelled to do it, why qualify it with a sense of value?

*

Words do something to reality. They mold it; they demonstrate the way you want it, the way you have it.

*

Poetry is a mental substance; or sexual (which is the same thing). You speak it with your cunt or your cock or your mouth or your asshole, or all of them. It's produced by sexual and mental energy.

*

Abstract terms are mostly suspect; they have been used vaguely and always to mean different things, obscuring all meaning. They have been repeatedly defined, never used for consistent purpose. Especially words (such as 'objective', 'subjective') which are one half of a pair of synonyms or opposites, are useless. Abstract language can, on the other hand, be used non-discursively. It often contains an exact relation to certain feelings which makes it ideal for description, creation, of those feelings. This is a painterly, non-grammatical use for the words.

*

When poems are read aloud, interpretation is a consequence of sympathy with the work. People who read their works well, testify to the interest of their writing.

*

In short poems it's hard to justify pushing all lines to the left, because it isn't necessary to continuously do that to control the poem. In a long poem it's useful to have that line for the eye and mind to travel quickly on.

*

The history of what's been done is a limit. It creates a feeling of possibility, that I don't like.

*

If the writer strains to do the work, it is more interesting.

*

The head contains myriad ideas. Structure provides an indication of the writer's sense of them.

*

Talk about poetry has at some point got to be abstract, in order to maintain itself in relation to the poetry. "I like this line here. I like this one." That isn't abstract. "Notice this rhyme here. See how this device works." That's not either. The talk becomes abstract when it is about these patterns of talk, of recognition, repetition, discourse.

*

Meaning changes when any different words are used (substituted or added). There are no two sets of words to say the same thing. This makes explanation very difficult, maybe impossible and worthless. You can either repeat what you said; or say something different, which can stand beside the first statement.

*

You can't speak and say nothing. Even images, say, are a kind of statement about something. All utterance is assertive.

*

It is necessary to let the mind go where it will in writing. The emotions lead it best. And things will be found and learned which otherwise wouldn't have been imagined.

*

Critical language should be direct. Like sonar it should aim itself at the object, what comes back will talk and close to accuracy.

*

Word *definitions* are scientific aspects of the language—utility. Poetry is everything else.

*

We talk of some words as abstract as opposed to concrete. This designation of difference is from *thinking*, where some things are of one context some from another. This doesn't pertain in *language, writing*. All words are abstract.

*

Writing, we fail at what we are doing. Our abilities are imperfect. But how do we have these imperfections? How do we face our work with them? The edge that is offered and used determines the cutting, the mark.

*

Each additional grammatical unit, each phrase, in addition to advancing the meaning, also has some amount of separation (distance) from what was written before. A question, for example, after a group of assertions, may be twice as far from those assertions as another statement would have been (though not necessarily). That is, all language has this quality of distance when used with other language.

*

Realize the huge distance between words; the arbitrariness of any grouping and configuration.

*

Words as we usually use them seem empty beside any mass of words used unusually. Use flattens words. Angles are gone out from between them. They need to be broken at some juncture and recombined.

*

(Any) great work in a medium advances the *instinct* for that work.

CLOSE READING CLOSE READING

A close reading is a reading made from within the mind of the person who wrote what is being read.

At some remove is a reading from within the words of the text. At one remove further, at the further removal of the one who reads, is the arena of the usual practice of reading.

It is the multiplicative modes of possible readings which make possible the inability to read, and the ability to read poorly. The ability to read well, to read closely, is thereby an ability developed within the mind, and an ability which remains there; the mind comes to grips with the mind; the text is its instrument; the other mind is its decisively imperfect and therefore instructional image of itself.

Reading, the activity of the mind upon itself, is not different from writing. If they are separated at all, it is by the uses we make of them, and the times in which we do it.

To read closely is to subtract from this distance, a distance which may be constituted only within the definitions, as they come to grammars, of the language, a distance which thereby exists; and in subtracting, to arrive at the origin of the text, the mind of the text in the mind of its writer. The text is a depository for the storage of the uses the mind has for the mind. It stores the implements whereby the mind works within and upon the mind, whereby the mind remains interior to the mind.

The interior is the region of the close, the mind is the region of the reading, and the point closest to the reading is the point of its productions.

The point of its production is the point of its production

within the mind, and within the mind of the world. A close reading of the text is a reading of the world, closer to the world if its text was written closer to its world.

The text survives the world in a reading of it, it survives the world of the text, because its writing was its subtraction from the deaths of its world. Reading the text resuscitates its world; reading it closely resuscitates the life of its world.

The close reading remains the auditor of that literature in which survive least the illusions of literature. The illusions of realism distract it, the illusions of narrative, the illusions of action. Close reading cannot ignore these habits where they do occur, but a premise of its closeness is their penetration.

Close reading practices the actions of the mind, not the habits of reading. Perhaps it could be called a readerly closeness, where readerly is not permitted to weaken it. Reading is actions of the text in the mind, but closeness implicates, within the mind, the actions of the mind. Close reading is not thought without actions, it is the actions of thought.

The situation demands the identity of action and thought.

Close reading is the necessary project of the mind in the presence of the text, vicinity of the text.

If there were no reason to read there would still be every reason to be close to the mind in thought.

The reason for reading is the excellence of the world. The reason for reading is its purification, its rigorous actualization, in thought. The reason for reading is the simplification of the acts and tenets of the world, the simple beauty of the text.

The entire effort of the mind is to get close to the mind. The multiple approaches to and through the mind lend their permissions to a variety of minds. Reading is of the variety of tools closest to the mind. The predilection of the mind for the mind, for the vocations of the mind, is the mind's choice. People choose otherwise; they choose to merely read.

A dissection of the text is not a close reading of it. The text dissects itself; that is one of the apparences wherein it lives. The dissection of a text is the activity of a shallow, overactive mind. The dissection of the text takes place in the region of the text, it is a product of a product. In producing out of the text, it produces the text as its product. The dissection of the text is nothing more than the pedagogical prerequisite of its dissemination.

The mind which reads closely is not so abstracted from itself as to require the assistance of this dissemination. The reading of the words of the text from within the words of the text is the activity of a mind at exercise, the activity of a mind which has not yet found its use, for itself, the activity of a mind separated from its acts.

Reading is a form of address wherein the writer, at the reader's insistence, addresses the reader. Close reading is a form of thought.

Understand each sentence as (a performance of) a mind at work. You will have begun to read.

Each mind has to realize the positive valence (value) of its constraints.

Closeness is body to body, also; body to body, with mind included.

So much understanding occurs in the verb that the meaning takes place in the mind.

Adjacent to the notion of close reading we must fabricate, in conclusion, a notion of close writing, which would be, to close reading, its agent, its abettor. Both exist exterior to the deniable portion of life, and are in fact its antidote, its denial.

A definition of close writing can be extrapolated. Close writing is the mind's use in, of, and for the mind, making use of an anticipated text, and of its own writing of that text. It is the close reading of the text, in advance, and, making possible all subsequent, it is the execution of thought which closes upon the purposes of thought.

If a blockage of the thought occurs in either the writing or the reading of the thought, it is not close; it is not close to itself.

The closeness is obtained by distancing, in distance. The longest aspect holds the truest thought.

ABUTTAL

One/1/　　Language encompasses writing, without any limit. Language is thinking prior to thoughts.

Reality encompasses the sets of each's all possible worlds. It is larger than the "all that we know to be the case," without limits.

Language, reality: two limitless worlds. Language plus or minus reality, reality plus or minus language, any factoring yields only confusion, confusion probably attended by fears.

The relationship between language and reality is not transitive. Neither takes the other as its object. Language, implementing a mind, tends to owningly grasp reality. This is an impossible, void action; it spreads mind through what it perceives as reality's interstices and "imperfections." Reality does not need language.

Language does not need reality. It is a peculiar perversion of poets to insist that it does. The proper province of language is language; its willed forays into reality are misguided, clumsy, fascistic.

Language and reality never touch. Using language as a tool to gesture in the supposed direction of reality is inconclusive; it does not need to happen. When it does, mind is required as a clean lever to return language to language. This latter activity of mind constitutes the indication of necessary writing, but for this the prior leasing of language toward reality is unnecessary. Language, at any moment an organized solid state of figments, is adequate to its own performance, in fact insisting on it. Any movement of language toward reality is a

retrograde movement; any writing out of such a movement is
retrograde writing.

One/2/   An indication of language's sufficiency will be
found in the mind's endless return to itself. Mind recalls mind.
Clarity is distance from reality. The longer vectors of thought
are sightings along shorter vectors of feeling, perception,
memory, intuition. The longest vector is language. The longest
vectors are the vectors of language. The guided pursuit of the
mind is towards its longest vector, language. There are no
equations, only the directions of directed insistent thought.
The longest distance between two intellected points, is
language.

Reality chops up the short distances, constitutively.
Reality can only fail language. There are no parabolas in this
discourse, no discourse; language returns to language, staying
there if we let it. We need to let it; we are dealing with an
intransigent matrix, transfers between the terms of which and,
moreso, transfers out of which, can only distract us from the
perseverant intransigence which it is our object to accept.

Mind's space is language. The temporal topological
space is reality's. No tautologies obtain between the "two."
Facts, truths, tautologies, are the possibility of language alone.

Language is substantive because it thinks. Reality
changes. Language does not think those changes. The changes
of language are implicit.

Language has no personalities, reality does. Lan-
guage need have no currency, reality must, *ipso facto*. The
insurgence of a language into, over, reality, is an effort to buy
what cannot be bought other than of itself instant to instant.
The instants of language are words (for example). There is
no possible relationship between any word and any instant
of reality. The perception of such a relationship, and any
writer's insistence upon it, is a passive perception thinking
itself complete. Time takes reality from reality, leaving reality.
Writing takes language from language, leaving language. Writing
is the diachronic function of language (a thinking clock which
does not stop).

Language does not perceive, neither does it

remember or forget, it does not imagine, it does not relate. Language writes. Language: the base upon which thought, mind, stand.

One/3/   There are spectacles that don't dominate anything. There is no reason for thought to influence reality. Reality needs the distance it demands from our attention.

One/4/   Language is the only function which can preclude thought. Reality is so easy to get to that ease is abolished; that language is abolished, made unnecessary. Thought is the mediator of distances between language. The use of language to mediate distances within realities is an excuse for thought. Thought *is* distance. If there was distance between language and reality it would have to be called what it is, a pervasive neurosis. Such imagined distances are overpermissive spaces; they evacuate thought of language, language of thought. The evacuation of language *of* language, is the excuse literature provides. This distance annotates an excursion into other time, a route the mind takes in losing language, the betrayal of the functional limits of either.

One/5/   Language starts to see others. It speaks. It writes stuff. It writes. It makes literature. It is literature. It is writing writing. It writes. It is language.

The others aren't others when language is language. Inverse proportion. Language is *the* substance which digests itself, openly. Each thing, each function, digests itself. Language does it with itself in the attention to the digestion of itself.

There are spectacles which don't take time because language is attendant to itself.

Two/1/   There is no reference not because there are no words but because there are no referents in language; not because there is no language but because there is no reality in language. Language doesn't make something that reality was. Language is not part of reality, can't perform it. Language doesn't leave anything out. There is no content. Neither language nor reality are adjectival in relation to the other; neither is judged, at all, in terms of "the other." Language and reality are separate organisms occupying the same space, the same time; the mind, in thought, is their mediator. Language suggests only itself. Tautology is its own mistake in assuming that near reflections can be reduced to a pointed perfection; the only equations are between times, and times are limits in motion.

Writing can't be a plural of reality. The language is exterior to an interior it won't suggest. Language is dimensionless; which permits writing. Dimensions talk only in speech. If there were a way to get from speech to writing it would be already divided. Speech is the unnecessary function of language, its reality; its necessary function is writing, is itself.

Writing merely carries language into an evaporative sense of reality. Time evaporates the connections. Language, using itself, evaporates them perfectly, not needing them. The mistaken attempt of writing has been to forge connections between language and reality. Language ages into (what) writing (has been) if it thinks itself in the presence of reality. When language occupies itself the world is complete. There is a distance between each thought which language occupies, motionless. Language endures as a disturbance its push toward reality. Thinking attached to reality is exactly this error.

When language is a semblance it is a semblance of its own reality; even there, badly. When language is alone, it thinks. This thinking language is the minimum of what writing must be. The higher denominators separate language from thought, without gain, without loss. When the language is the language, thought and reality will take their own inventing and invented courses.

Two/2/   Writers experience the excellent tools of their minds; in producing the products of those tools, they don't stop to demand that they give, rather, those tools to the reader. In providing the tools, a writer provides a working which the reader then practices. The tools obtain an even exchange between writer and reader. The work is an embodiment of the tools which provides the tools. An emphasis on craft, on texture, on things having to do with the surface of the work, on its appearance, is evidence that an object is being presented, shown, sold, instead of the active offering of tools for making.

Writing must offer its tools without the encumbrances of their having been used. Clean tools.

Two/3/   Writing is preferentially a moment whose idea has come.

This transfer is automatic if the tools are furnished perfectly. And if the tools are furnished excellently the time is erased in their, in its, accuracy; it doesn't speak itself because it becomes embodied without body in the tools of a mind's excellence. It is manifestly a mind which forgets its mind in thinking writing. And the triumph remains in the integers of thought, that they forget themselves from experience in order to enunciate without object, without obstacle.

Two/4/   Writing wants sentences that don't have too many uses. Writing, a refinement of language in the direction of thought, wants sentences that don't have too many uses. Reality has too many uses.

Literature is what time remembers as writing at its best. Literature is the mistake time makes of writing. Time has too many uses.

Two/5/   The critical function compares a literature with literature, a writing with writing, a language with language. The function of philosophy is the stringent comparison of a reality with reality, with realities. The imperfection of philosophy — that it makes its report in language, that even logic is not its exclusive province — is an indication of literature's justified aloofness as it writes, provided it remains inside itself. The preeminent value of literature, of writing, is that it is the only discourse which may speak itself and, in fact, to be preeminent, to preempt, it must do entirely that.

Three/1/   Language is a just instrument.

Its cleavage of the moment is perfectible.

It can be made to utter perfectly.

It doesn't carry a name. It cleaves one. It isn't an authorship, it cleaves one.

This latter function, language's active surveillance of the mind, makes the mind go forward, makes language perfectible.

The mind sharpens its own tools in sharpening language. The language is then sharpened with the mind's sharpened tools.

A mind that sees its language sharpening reality, a mind that sees itself sharpening reality with language, inverts the perfectibility of language. A mind performs no more than a stunt in gesturing toward reality with language. If language leaves the mind with reality as its object, however partial or obscured, it leaves behind its extant perfection and its latent perfectibility. In seeking an arena for its operations outside the arena which makes its operations act, language makes a mess for consumption. Language does not destroy itself in leaving the mind, not even that interest: language destroys itself in leaving language, but it may do this only within the mind, the place where its constraint is noticed.

The mind can only make language lamely contingent on reality; it can't make any relationship obtain. This is a limit which language profitably poses upon the mind; in writing, it seeks the mind.

Three/2/   Thought precedes writing but it does not precede language. Writing which assumes thought, i.e., which need not pause in passing through thought, can reach language directly. If it is peculiarly excellent it can present this direct approach directly through the reader to the locale of the reader's thought. If the mind's language is strong enough its writing is that language. In such a demonstration writing in effect bypasses itself: language addresses language.

One/1/   It is an annihilative function of language which presumes to collect its mind's assumption of reality. A mind's broadest possible distribution of language, and throughout itself, instant to instant, is its fathomable success. From within, language sees reality as a sum of dispersing languages. This induction of reality as pluralizing languages is a mistake, which the mind enjoys for its easy safety: language's recognition of languages is a perception entirely internal to language. Writers in particular are too willing to make of their language an overvoracious reader of reality. Language properly writes, itself.

One/2/   There is no reason to go to language to look for reality.

If language and reality face each other they die. There is no distance and there is too much distance. Speaking is a sort of intermediary, a second in a nonexistent duel.

There would be no proof of the equation sketched here: but writing exists. Writing is the actions language makes if it acts with only itself in mind.

There is nothing to be lost. Language preserves itself. Mind preserves itself. Reality preserves reality.

The loss is in the aberrant associations. Each appetite adequately preserves itself. Some (mind and language) cooperate. This shortens the unlikely distances of time, reduces them from an equation to a reflex.

Language makes no mistake, persists, in finding in mind its location.

Language doesn't fabricate anything: it doesn't make reality, it doesn't make mind. Language doesn't fabricate. Language is a function: much more than a sign of a sign (it doesn't "stop"). Language is an impervious sign, one that operates. Language has a direction if the mind pushes it. If it pursues reality, it pursues.

"   ". This is reality. An exchange which it is easy to make. The appearance of solid objects is "solid." Language punctuates itself with excellence.

Two/1/   Language penetrates language.

If you view (them as) integers in space, you view (them as) time. Time is the failure in thinking which exists (to fill the area) between language and reality.

Subtracting reality from language is subtracting time from language. Time does not belong as a component of either.

The = sign is a sequence in time. It renders even the tautology at least a distance and a direction, a duration. You make the time be a factor.

Two/2/   History and memory are equally fabric. So is language. Language is the most powerful. Its misuse is an epidemic. Language's power is control. It makes itself (be in) control by thinking. Language allows the distances perceived in time to be a matter of thought. It is the equation, of any sort, between language and reality, that makes of this a mess in thought. This equation is persuasive because it is palpable: this constitutes its persuasion. Language pollutes reality when it is the tool of entry. Properly, language remains a closed ecological system, the one in which we think.

Two/3/   History is more dimensional than reality. Language's obsession with the obsessive languages of reality serves stiffly to prop this up. Language's obsession with language's language, the mind's equator, serves equitably. History is a loose denominator in the game; it escapes notice, it happens later.

Two/4/   Language does not think backwards, it does not think forwards. Language is nowhere diachronic. History is a mistake the mind makes in thinking it remembers through language.

Language is a simple structure. When reality takes sides through language it is the fault of language. But language is properly impervious to fault. There is a relationship which language wishes to produce; the relationship with language, the relationship productive of writing.

If there isn't a way in which time "talks to" reality, there is no language. There is no language mistake. And language was language and there is no time.

There is a moveable quotient in the element of thinking that language is. It is immoveable within itself. If language thinks of itself it thinks well. If language thinks in a direction, it passes.

There is no history because there is no noun and no verb. There *is* a predicate with a solidity. There are actions which take place; the actions within language: all, appear, to be.

There is language, an integer with an integer to be.

If you have to do something do it with language because language is complete. Style.

Apropos of the world it is a fact that it doesn't speak.

Two/5/   Language is a nominator. It controls. Time wastes time redundantly.

Language exhausts the mind's will to write. Time can't be wasted, not even in this pursuit. The relationship of language to time is a relationship assumed in hasty perception.

Language is the only adequate substance, a function language demands of the mind, of mind's reality. This function makes writing.

Two/6/ Language does nothing with time. The diachronic fracture of language is fictitious: both mistakes. The notion that history, teaches, is a retrograde function of language, language still in search of itself. There are no apologetics for language; that is its history, its allure, its drive; its writing.

Languages takes its time. It does not fill it. It does not empty it. It takes it. It gives it. Language permits time because permission is a sanction language demands of itself. When language admits time it forgets for itself as imperfectly as the conclusive language perfectly forgets for itself.

Language is not a declinable subject. It is a function which will not be declined. The temporal declensions of time are failures of thinking which turn on themselves.

There is a language which languages. It is the positive, the only, writing. Literature resuscitates in being language; otherwise it is a perfunctorily over-adequate gesture.

Language ceaselessly recognizes its moment without accepting it, without denying it. This would seem to imply, to implicate, time. Language's recognition in writing is the first adequate writing, the premier language.

If language wanted to talk to time it would write. If it wanted to write it would forget time.

Three/1/ The mind is a collector of information: that is its premier function.

The gathering of information is a simple inelegant process prior to thought. Perception, the organism's gathering of information, is a simple inelegant process propaedeutic to its mind's use of those perceptions. An effort to place language in relation with perceived reality is a cumbersome and meddlesome effort to patch up the distance extant between perception and mind. The effort provides in the patch an image of the distance, widening it; it is in the faulty obliqueness of the apperception that language looks "back," turns from itself, loses (itself). Language assumes the initial distance between perception and thought as an error, an error immediately and at length devastatingly corrosive of language. Language's position within this situation provides an image of distance, but its position there is unnecessary; in providing an image of distance language presents it as a discrepancy, (a valuation, and) one which does not exist. The distance between perception and thought is a measuring of thought by perception, of perception by thought: each is, is constant. When language trespasses, even briefly, it breaks the constancy of an already complete equation.

Language is its own equation, complete in one term.

Three/2/   We can't intuit intentions from the facts of the world. We mustn't replace them with our own.

Language doesn't intend anything. It isn't a reason for anything. Language is not a specimen of thought: it is the tool using which thought thinks; it is a functioning specimen of thinking.

(And there is no history in this latter statement; there is a grammar, of points. It is an unintentional grammar of signs. The signs motivate their own direction in (any consciousness of) the position(s) they already maintain.)

Intention is motivated by the fear that something will happen, by the knowledge that something will happen. Knowledge becomes fear if it intends. Each integer of speculation is a lost integer. The language intends itself by being used. When a writer intends language to intend, the writer bends it twice; the writer's first intention, to do so, fails to show the language, fails because it has shown itself twice already, its doubled intending in language.

"The brevity of life is a brief language": does not imply that language is brief; language is as extensive as its work. The work, in particulars, must be as extensive as language, must not evaporate of itself, through intention, into ego/memory/

history/time. Gestures of history and thought evaporate out of time; it is language which heats them in durable heat. Thought travels at the speed of language; it can't be pushed beyond that speed by intention or below that speed by history.

One/1/   Q: What does there have to be for there to be meaning?
             A: Language.
             Q: What does there have to be for there to be reality?
             A:
The question does not make sense. An answer to it would of necessity occur in language. An answer to it would have jumped systems or, perhaps more exactly, from a world to a system. Reality is the system which doesn't answer its own questions.
             Language is the system which does. A language is a system which does.
             There is no question of a distance between language and reality. (It is the province of language to ask of itself its distances (that is how it advances), and of writing to do so excellently.) There is no equatability, no difference. There is no relationship. When we construe one we confuse functions, what we then do is not even meaning, it has no relation to meaning. Meaning is in the province of language. Any effort to make it obtain for reality is a failure in language, and a failure for all meaning.
             Thought doesn't "fail" in reality. It isn't there. It is through language that thought's meaning is incessant.
             Every success in thinking is a success in language: a furtherance. We can't know (what) a success in reality (would be).
             Language is centered on the thought of thought. Reality is acentric (that is why we fix points within it).
             You can't think reality and language at the same time. You can only think language.
One/2/   Reality has no limit. Language has a limit, and we see this in its grammar, its possible syntaxes, in its use. Lan-

guages have a limit, because when we think of a plural of
language we do so from the point of view of reality, a realm
where these very plurals constitute our sense of its limitless-
ness.

One/3/   The particular instances of language are limits.
But language has no limit because it is in motion. Its motion
is described in grammar. And its motion is limited by style,
the production of a grammatical particular.

One/4/   Language isn't, is it, there. Reality is a constantly
questionable pantheon in this universe of noun verb relation-
ships. Mind is a constant, thought its active endeavor. The line
between language and anything else is crooked: indicative
enough. Language is the (only) un-metered control. Language is
reality without excuses. The excuses are literature. The language
is an articulable realm, i.e., a realm with its "own" realm.
Language measures the distance between two thoughts; the
distances between realities is unmeasurable, a quotient without
factors.

There is a space in which language operates which
is inoperable in terms of reality. The shortest distance between
two points is the abolition of those points. Language. When
time blows into a parameter of distances, that is reality; when
time *flows*, language. Language doesn't make mistakes. Nor is
there an excuse for reality. And reality is the ignorant sequence
of events, ignorant of place. It specializes. Language stops. If
language didn't, *precisely*, surround us we wouldn't specialize,
time would stop.

Language mediates the space between thought.

Language opens only into the unquestionable
realm of language.

There is no time. Thinking "reality" only manages
to fabricate time. Language subtracts this mistake. Language
subtracts the mistake of history, of memory: language subtracts
reality into language, without reality.

One/5/   A relation between language and reality is a surplus
value of the mind's consumption of reality.

The consumption of the surplus is what has usually
been literature. Writing, and very much against that, must be

the consumption of language in language. Writing: the assumptions of language in language.

If language were to purchase reality, it would "be worth something." Language's valuation of *itself* is what writing is, what literature will be.

A relationship between language and reality is equivocal.

One/6/   If there is a pretended distance between language and reality it is the distance organized in plot; plot is a misnomer for time which language fabricates when its mind makes it approach reality. When this plot infuses "thinking," thinking stops.

If there is an appearance it is an appearance of language. Only language appears. Other worlds revolve, evolutively. The time it takes language to approach reality is time lost to the mind. The mind doesn't lose time; language loses time if it approaches reality. Language can only disdain reality: an object which only language can pretend to be a (its) object.

One/7/   There is no distance. Language. Reality. There is no distance to be bridged. The distance is something mind slips between language and reality in an erratic effort to make itself stable. There is no balance which can be accomplished between language and reality. The two are isolate: to say more, to say even that, is to try to unite them.

There are eras, and that does not constitute writing. Writing is a constituent assembly of language, and that is all.

There *is* a distance to be constituted. It is the distance between thought and thought. Language, in its function, constitutes this distance. And it is not a distance; it is language.

MODES

Speak instantly...

Is it still possible to speak of *the* world,
after reading this?

with authority...

end of the world. end of a life.
          (punctuation)

each word's...

Strain every word particle-fibre.
*
The verb particles in every word.
*
In relation words swell or diminish.
The fluctuation's meaning.

concerted working.

paralogical statements
*
Using words; hold stringently to degree of force, vector, weights
moved, direction (movement off previously-established lateral
plane, etc), constantly new vista with each sentence...phrase...
breath!, the electrical charge used and that emitted, what is con-
trolled and what given.

(Strange, need metaphor to talk of the speech activity;

        Also, that it becomes, like, idealistic; talk of enlightenment.

        Impossible totally doing this. Get close via refined attention correlative with say solitude; not there.

— No external authority.

Write clear; space required like blank page.
Again, solitude.
Have to move over the entire white; then write. Absolute choices, one after another and together, to make any and what parts black. Importance of the *design* of a work; holds the pattern of choices, to blacken. More important than meaning or intention.

        Space already part filled, charcoal on patches of page. Must write around those areas, or clear through them. Very difficult to obtain 'the whole thing clear' to work in. (Mallarmé, closest

        Sense of *a* life inevitable, because of unclear areas. Clear language writing thus *partly* possible.

        Undisturbed attention, clear itself, gets on.

Speaking instantly with authority each word's concerted working. — No external authority.

U N A D O R N E D ca 78

Karl Kraus:
In these great times, which I knew when they were small,
which will again be small if they have time, and which because
in the field of organic growth such transformations are not
possible, we prefer to address as fat times and truly also as
hard times; in these times when precisely what is happening
could not be imagined, and when what must *happen* can no
longer be *imagined*, and if it could it would not happen; in these
grave times that have laughed themselves to death at the
possibility of growing serious and, overtaken by their own
tragedy, long for distraction and then, catching themselves in
the act, seek words; in these loud times, booming with the
fearful symphony of deeds that engender reports, and of
reports that bear the blame of deeds; in these unspeakable
times, you can expect no word of my own from me. None
except this, which just preserves silence from misinterpret-
ation. Too deeply am I awed by the unalterable, is language
subordinate to misfortune. In the empires bereft of imagin-
ation, where man is dying of spiritual starvation while not
feeling spiritual hunger, where pens are dipped in blood and
swords in ink, that which is not thought must be done, but
that which is only thought is inexpressible. Expect from me
no word of my own. Nor should I be capable of saying any-
thing new; for in the room where someone writes the noise is
so great, and whether it comes from animals, from children,
or merely from mortars shall not be decided now. He who
addresses deeds violates both word and deed and is twice
despicable. This profession is not extinct. Those who now have

nothing to say because it is the turn of deeds to speak, talk on.
Let him who has something to say step forward and be silent!

active entity

performing language writing
                    N.P. & A.D.

Life consists / Of propositions about life.
Stevens, Men Made Out of Words

Without Thinking

Segal's people are somnambulists. People empty of person.
Stoppingly stark, chokes, barely.

Twombly
to absorb the information ⊠
Or holding on to the quantities
instant morsels arted in
the back of the cave in color
with color
the fascination or the snow
the cage momently cloggeded
when the faces
economy of gesture by profuse think
stop, let stop time
measure of order between thought
or the distance from M*é to D*i

or and writing fought
while the meanwhile course of past
parcelly impress present, to
the the the the welter
whirrs in by vases word
comparable to the in mason
the wading figure
stubborn before struck, mouthe
mover or the waves armor
as the so is the, or almost
the body or for the wall
time with the work for it
casually not so or at all
harness in the thin labial wax
the letter from the area
an old story ahead to the past
gradually the quickest movement
a vertical order of the days
signature the blind heading
space abatingly sets by
space with heat by the time
decides hangs stuffs
so that it away in
organ in spoken, in punctuate
positions the base
in time of time allied with pace
numbers to slowly start
bilingual caution, erasure
value or the murk for
this gentle of passion device
numbers to thinkes
th'or duplicity for zones
decisively shift handed
patience of the eye to load that
the back, the mind's plunge
the margin for error, right
a heave of feathere
square light by angle at

of affinity for its muted
the lawn beneath the weedling
a limit the words
peaceforcefull individual thoughts
fold in the neatening less
flailing skirts in attend
weavess throws on blessing
the leaf of the maker in thrall
faltering no ceaseless furtherance
faultless no, or undertaken
throws on the salten pettles

There are two words near in sound which describe this show: calligraphic and cacographic (the urge of each for completion of the other).

There is a difference between what is necessary and what is understandable, and that difference is filled by what happens.

If you write a line at a time, you must balance the line.

In film, the drawing occurs with light, the narration with color. Sound is a distortion of this simplicity.

She was reading the words.
She had the words memorized.

The production quality of a book is the first critical attention it receives.

When you leave a major road for a minor one, *that* is a language detour.

Structural Similarities of Singularity

We temper our words with speech our thoughts with air In being here to be there

Ego is easier to lose than aura.

You can only measure the acceleration of change if you measure it against something that doesn't accelerate. And where would you get that which doesn't accelerate; against what would you measure it.

It's easy to say that it's a better grasp on structure because the structures are larger. Too easy.
The moment's attention, locked to any sound from inside any word:— that structure must locate itself from within and without, in relation to such points.

Knowing how the distortions travel through the system, makes it possible to cut out the distortions.

An assertion which contains each of its terms as the object of what it asserts, which predicates them, whose object is its (sic) terms; which, treads for the exact duration of its exacted terms in combination.

I am writing what I am getting ready to write.

Each the conductor of another's train...

$$\frac{\text{politics}}{\text{art}} = \text{politics}$$

$$\frac{\text{art}}{\text{politics}} = \text{art}$$

Writings requisite mind mind coordination.

and to you mea culpa
the processionless bonds of
this intimacy

"The sentence is the passage from one point of thought to another point of thought. This passage is achieved in a thinking sleeve."
Michaux, Ecuador

At work upon the paradoxes, one finds that all effort is waste upon itself.

irrespondence

A tautology is a tautology.

A contradiction is not a contradiction.

The Machine Which Makes (My) Writing
‖
autobiography, an

The product of the creative process is a specific ideational-aesthetic content actualized in linguistic material in which both content and material form a dialectical unity.
Jiří Levý

Language writes writing. A writer is the instrument of language. The writer has written the writer.

Anything typed presumes the character of a typed page. One letter, placed, presupposes the entire design. The design is a product of the machine. The typed writing is a byproduct.

/Type*written*: the sign for this mistake./

Yet our reading habits make, in our mind, of the lines of the page, *a* line. The historic thus gets implied out of a basically unhistoried, frequently unintentional, choice of implement.

This dialectical imbalance poisons the typing act. The letters perform, of machinative necessity, outside the ambiance of unsullied thought. They share the space of an unreconciled act.

Literary magazines should have as their goal the emptying of the world of speech.

What I am endeavoring to write is what we have all most recently forgotten. But don't mistake me, I am not a rememberer.

Simple statements are often based on language fears, and sometimes result in dogma or non-sense.
Robert Smithson

Everything we know, which is to say everything we can do, has finally been turned against what we are.
Valéry

Take it back.
I can't.
It's been used.
Don't run.

Everything means something which the world predisposes it to mean.

Language.
            Everywhere.→

When she was having a bad day she couldn't tell the difference between an addition sign and a multiplication sign because they both went around and around in circles.

We only wait for the words to gather dust of our thought.

The glue is not the sonata.

AUDITORY CRYSTAL

"Don't forget to take out the structure."

"An immense machine produces waste matter from the discourse of the west."
Julia Kristeva

Sleeping/Dreaming
It probably has to do with perception: the horizontal is more easy to obtain than the vertical.
Waking/Dreaming

+

The drawings are all anatomy. The machines are all machines.

A war draws women. The direction is split. It all is found.

Can the pumps help the fat?

"Thought is too small."

Beuys in Willoughby Sharp videotape

    +

Everyone watches someone draw in this puffy mist.

autophilogy

"Interest in an intensified form can lead to love."
Beuys

Genius is an ability to forget for a moment you know every-
thing.

"Art is the understanding of labor in the different fields of
creation."
Beuys at Cooper Union

Joseph Beuys: temperament is a democratization of the word
'art.'
    Mr. Beuys' program is his constant verbing of the noun 'art.'

The words "signifier" and "signified" are both signifiers.

The sound isn't in the diction. It's in the thought.

The "poem in the old sense of the word" is distinguished by a
syntax of utterance, of its utterability.
    For the text there is, as against the unutterable, a readerly

passion.

Positive negative: a syntax in relation.

Nonsyntactic (apparel) — a form of (formal) violence contra the carefully (dressed).

Two pails

Two combs

horizontals as vertical, The.

verticals as horizontal, The.

In place of syntax?
Works.

A change in perception stays there.
    The writing can remain to appear the same.

When you start to think in sentences, — critic.

You must have the wherewithal to test it.

Vocabulary is crucial. Any art is ascendant only in the *production* of vocabulary, and not in productions out of it.

Nervous breakdown, cathartic overload. This makes syntax make sense.

Assignations of sense: — this makes a mistake in the thinking.

Each word is its own only limit. They are not limited, touched, by contingency with anythings other.

Perhaps elevated language is in consequence of a unity of the "two" subjects (speaking subject, spoken subject), the identity of these "this". Such nonschizophrenic utterance approaches the textual locale in this, that the potential languages are made one unity, and differs from it primarily in the utterance making its, itself, apparent.

The performance of a model of reality is (my) aesthetic.

I believe in a tautological universe.

A relationship between language and experience is always impoverished. The latter is poor. Language only gains on experience when it is experience. To do this, it must absolutely relinquish, must negate (as zero the integers) experience.

The degree to which the mystery/(*aura*) comes from a person-
ality and not the language, is the degree to which the work fails.

UNATTRIBUTED ca 79

end sound	first sound
end word	end word

end sound	first sound
first word	first word

common	uncommon
common	common

common	uncommon
common	uncommon

STORY

numeral characters

he $_1$
she $_4$
they $_{1,3,4,7}$
(for instance

(ambiguous character
he $_{1 \text{ or } 3}$
they $_{4 \text{ or } 7, 1 \text{ or } 3}$

art unescapably mnemonotechnical

Proust, Beckett, Stein

"It was as if some barbarous somnambulists had mumbled in the daytime the bizarre atrocity of their thoughts."
Romance Conrad/Hueffer

probable vectors—

prone; vertical; lateral

LeWitt
exhaustive
persistent
obsessive
simple
:quatrain (agoraphobic delineate)

I confess that a certain use of the imperative indicative — that cruel tense which represents life to us as something ephemeral and passive at the same time, which at the very moment it retraces our actions stamps them with illusion, annihilating them in the past without leaving to us, as the perfect tense does, the consolation of activity — has remained for me an inexhaustible source of mysterious sadness.
Proust *On Reading* footnote 3

With the use of two words — of; and — a writer can control half of whatever he can make unusual. In relationship; in combination.

Then, how to do it without them — the less easily chartable excitement.

At 3 a.m. I awake from a dream, which continued as I became awake, of prose lines tumbling and interlocking.

Lines of prose already set within margins, moved over each

other; all the even-numbered lines were moving down one line. The new ordering of lines: 1,3,2,5,4, etc. There was then a gap of greater space between the first and third lines; all the other lines were more tightly knit than previously.

Coexistent with this vision, was one of a more fluid moving and recombining of the lines. Of this latter, apart from its sensuality, I retain only the image of an eyehook as a device protruding through certain lines of the prose, perhaps the device for linking and holding the final arrangement.

(I can't sleep now)

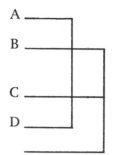

B/C synthesis

prolonged description (abstracted optically; through mucous state) of non-experienced place, e.g. desert

achieve pre-literate mind: use literacy as tool not end

A world of nouns and verbs is latent, bored. The modifiers are the activity, the movers; meaning can hardly be said to begin without their titillation.

the morphe juste

a word;
inscribes
its affect

I said glottal. Charles said you mean clotted. I had wanted to use glottal and have it *work* as clotted.

zen — no transitive verbs

practice makes practice

object(the words)ivist

long work the force of which is its function, device: one morph

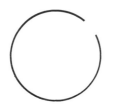

In to it? Out of it? No. I make my thoughts.

novel:
all words from the notes,
should be spoken in the novel
        (brief novel)

from Stein, *Mrs. Reynolds*, last page last sentence, 1942 — There is nothing historical about this book except the state of mind.

Proceed by emasculation. Each subsequent statement releasing the previous into unexpected, unlikely, space.

In a text each word is photonic = its chance of being there, its chance of going further.

A text which allows only "horizontal" words. One which permits only "vertical" words. A text which screens out both; here the words must have no aspect of light about them.

"...the mouth is only a movable and answering ear..."
Novalis

There is what else is there than this death of verbs.

We look into each others' eyes and correct each other's minds.

Distance between the verbs is equal to $27 \div X = N$
(where $X = N$)

Subjects A & B begin simultaneously and intersect. Follow A to the intersection, then B; keep both always equally forefront and apparent.

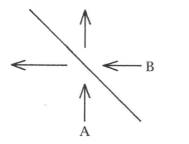

                                                    ?³

Lead the idea in pursuit of its affable structure.

Structure is sense. The working will be obtained.

Write in the space of a thought.

<u>book</u>
  0

Criticism functions to the definition of its terms. The rest is discourse.

structure cubes words

words^3 ⌐

      structure

Make a text in which the letters will appear to move (progress) from the right margin to the left.

Answers to metaphysic questioning are abstract. The mark the sign of the pursuit is diffuse.

Q:
A: Literature.
Q:
A: Words.

If the reader is facing north then the word "the" is a vertical opaque surface tilting toward the space between east-northeast and northeast.

$$\frac{\text{politics}}{\text{art}} = \text{politics}$$

$$\frac{\text{art}}{\text{politics}} = \text{art}$$

$$\left\{ \begin{array}{l} \dfrac{p}{a} = p \\[2ex] \dfrac{a}{p} = a \end{array} \right.$$

$$\left\{ \begin{array}{l} a = \dfrac{p}{p} \\[2ex] p = \dfrac{a}{a} \end{array} \right.$$

$$a = p$$

Private Enigma in the Opened Text

The trace of the enigma is negligently latent in all writing. The enigma is a colorless monovalent feature in textual omnivalence.

This present writing defines those private enigmas with which the author sometimes pierces his text. These are distinct from, for example: the narratively enigmatic which, functioning, becomes through reappearance, a character or figure of the text; the metaphysically enigmatic which functions, deliberately, through our lives as we return to its imperative point of question; the enigmatics of dream which function, vehicularly, to let life ride itself; the grammatically enigmatic, which functions as a verbal irregularity, a non sequitur stunning us with what previously could not have been said; the enigmatic of any single text, which is obsessive in its function as the ground for all text and all enigma. Throughout this writing, the word 'enigma' will refer to private enigmas, and not to the otherwise enigmatic which may frequently surround its appearance.

The author may plant in his text his enigmas. Whether this is more common in the rangeingly modern text than in classical writing is something we may not learn. We may speak of the pleasure. The writer allows his enigmas as, quickly they choose him; with reason—pleasure. The attachment is attentive. There is pleasure in placing the deliberately extraneous, the stain. The enigma may be no more enigmatic to a reader than is the rest of the text, which may seem 'of a piece', or deliberately and equally not of one. But for the writer, the enigma remains a sign of himself in the text of himself, a unique entry of himself upon his language. It is that part which he obstinately holds to as he gives it all away. The presence of the reader is implicit in the pleasure of enigma; the author is a voyeur, enjoying as he writes, the pleasure of his reading of his text. In fact, he gives the text to himself as he writes it: but in the enigma he claims in one instant the combined functions of reading and writing; he completes already, again and in part, what already others, reading, complete again and in part. He enjoys, in advance, what it is usually for the reader, whether himself or another, to enjoy only later. It is one-sided pleasure; doubled. The enigma is chosen as a special burden, a verdict the writing passes on the young history of text.

The enigma cleans the text of its indebtedness. In the enigma gesture, a text lays hold of itself. An enigma, unlike the rest of texted language bound to structure, does not (have to) evaluate itself. It is already evaluated, it stands for that.

What is sought is an enigma which cannot be closed upon (hence the "is sought"). Small particles of meaning satisfy this best for the writer; though large structures do so, openly, they do so as structures, their closure a matter of preordained interest. The enigma is erased in its minute duration. An enigma, unlike the rest of structured text, is not the locus of any coming together, neither of a dispersion; it is a still point activated, once by the author's enthusiasm, and again by the writing which surrounds and which motivated its inauguration. Enigma, made to be unresolved, affords the opposition of immersion, of argument: it offers an opaque exterior; not offering entry or exit, it posits (the generic trace of pleasure). The enigma, cued only to itself, faces nothing. However, it is not bracketed. It is merely less loose among particles more active. Though its delight is not extinguished, it has no tendency. Its argument is that, it, is, here; hence its relation to structural wholes: the enigma less elusive, because more instanced, the structure less clear, because more over itself.

The enigma significantly animates (animates signification in) the writer's working. In his text he lodges it, stills the agitation by posturing its particular particle where it can be observed, contemplated, or where it can be passed over; without having to reveal its lived significance, he reveals the volume of it. It is transplanted; without, however, having been anywhere other than on both sites, met equally in the imagination with which they touch. The enigma is rendered siteless, a vantage from which its singularity can incite unanimously.

The enigma is the only anoegenetic particle of language. It stands, in part (and in part it 'fails'), for the effort which made it so. It does not sublimate its function to structure, as do all functioning chunks of meaning; it is apart from function, embodying it at once. It is an action on which the curtain of meaning has come down with finality; behind the curtain, the perfunctory disclosure of fact. The enigma is a silent spot in the rush of meanings, but only when viewed in that context. Its placement specializes it. Without being able to deposit its position in the meaning-productive text, it does in fact speak its stance. It refuses to speak in discourse in order to embody quick monologic impact.

The enigma is impoverished in context. It has nothing to do: no work, nothing by which to be covered, nothing to speak, no acts, no decisions to make or motivate in its place (no pivot), no early nor late and no here nor there. It has nothing to mobilize (after the author's delight), nothing to solve, nothing to begin or bring to an end. It abolishes, for an instant, what goes on surrounding it. If a text can be parsed, the enigma cannot. But it does not deny, it solidly confirms itself; its intractable dissolution of logic and sequence. But it must not irritate; it is in no way entangled. It is not a version of some other thing, neither is it averse to a possibility. It is stopped. It implies the release of the game, momentarily, without bringing it about. It generates its instant, and deprives it of reason, of play.

The enigma does not exist in the tangled limits of nature. It is an artifact. It in no way approaches the limits of what we know to be the case. It stands (in) (in the text) for the limits. It is an act of indication, but without the masking words which elsewhere accompany such acts; its substance is word, but it leaps, releasing them insoluble, an empty encasement. The enigma is marked by its absence from the site, as it is seen to occupy it totally. No contradiction; this, the enigma.

An enigma cannot be plural; it depends upon its indistributability. If it becomes dispersed in the text, if it is acted, its character is delineated in diffusion; of necessity, its still factness is destroyed. When the integer is serialized, or valued, when it is perceived through horizontal or vertical loci, it achieves a rhetorical or narrative function; it relaxes. The enigma must not be made to speak itself in any direction. The enigma, if it is to stand privately, if it is to release its pleasure, must not equivocate. The enigma is the only detached attachment permitted to text.

A text can be infused with a network of enigmas, which unavoidably connect. But when the enigma is extensive, it becomes a particle in the text's fabric, a code demanding, and enabling at least in part, its decipherment. As soon as an enigma is extensive, structured, it becomes a term among many in the text's polarities and excursions. It becomes one of numerous graphs upon which the writing occurs, tightening and loosening. Its dissolution proposes its solution; it talks. And it is no longer private; the text has begun to reply. The enigma is not permissive.

The enigma is consigned, ordered. It is the object of an action which, as a singularly upright subject, it demands. Unlike all other text, the enigma needs no support. It does not need to be there. It seems to be a will, to embody will so completely, that its it is embodied. It is irreversible. An order that cannot be recalled, it cannot die: its allure. The enigma is messageless; perfectly balanced (of one 'side'), it is the perfect signifier, the only one not drawn apart (revealed) by unequal (metaphorically inexact) sides. Stolid, it doesn't waver.

SKIN

This is a talk about two grammars. Sex and film. This is a talk about two American grammars.

An indication of the relationships, and also, and differently, of the relations, between these two gestural grammars, is evident within the words *skin* and *film*.

film 1. A thin *skin* or membraneous coating.
skin 3. Anything resembling skin in function or appearance; any outer layers, accretion, or protection, such as the rind of fruit, the surface *film* on boiled milk, or the plating on a ship or rocket.

This beginning has been made only to establish the two words within the probable relationship within which they are, as is already evident, the scenic texture of life as it is lived in the bedroom and the screening room. It is interesting to note that both such rooms are habitually, though not always, darkened prior to these very special indulgences. In the screening room, a light comes from behind and above our heads and onto the screen of our experiences. It might be said, metaphorically, to do so in the bedroom. In the sexual acts which the bedroom so commonly circumscribes, and inscribes, the brilliances of our experiences come into our eyes and into our bodies within those special postures which sex obtains for them. It might be said, metonymically, that we live similarly in the screening room, where the special relationship and posture of the body to an object of light is, after all, so essential to that experience.

In these and related, and relating, ways, it is postures within frames, at least of reference, which hierarchize within these gestureful acts the words, graphs, sequences and propositions, the facts of our living within them, the impossibility, for us, of our living without them.

Within the filmic discourse, and by that is not meant this, or any other, talking about it, but within that discourse which itself encompasses in its actions, the maker and the viewer enter into a discourse, intercourse. The maker caresses the viewer with images, the viewer caresses the maker with attentions and, frequently, with money. In sex acts, the participants are, first of all, attendant to one another's image, each being, within waves of alteration, a viewer or a maker, or, a viewer and a maker. Each caresses the other with images and with that ecstacy resident within the memory as fund of images, but usually not, at least not directly, with money. Perhaps money inscribes these two regions of bliss, that is of simultaneous remembering and forgetting, into an inverse ratio of proportions; perhaps the payment of money for the pleasures of film forms a percentage whose inverse is that percentage formed by the frequency of payment for sex. We must see that this indicates the unity, within our culture, of these two gerunds, of their several gerunds, in that each subtracts, at least in the sphere of the two made obvious, conversely from our funds of money. This balance which, simply, is the one which we have attacked first, is balanced by several emphases and harmonies, among which: for the one we are clothed, for the other naked, for the one we open our eyes, closing them infrequently, for the other we may frequently close our eyes, occasionally opening them, for the one we most commonly sit and for the other most commonly do not, for the one we most always leave home, for the other more commonly not, into each we make a penetration and in each we are penetrated, each we engulf, as each engulfs us, and in each we make in order to be unmade.

There are various distortions which we willingly tolerate in order to see, to think, and to live, more clearly. It is necessary that we carry into these experiences some current versions of our clarities in order that we leave those experiences with an at least somewhat multiplied version of those clarities which we live in order to enhance, that our aggravations seem to us to be somewhat less than necessary, and our clarity somewhat more than more. Thus, and this has been simply to say that, in each the duplicities or our involvement will necessarily divide only to then impact into that whole within which alone it is possible that we continue to live. Whether we sit still or move about a little, whether we move with attention to those movements and are but occasionally still, we must acknowledge that we are within situations that we have made, that we are within situations that have been made for us, but that it is precisely the separation of these distinctions, our recognition of them, in them, which destroys them for us, and which destroys, more furtively if one chooses not to recognize it, the digital identity of either or any of us within these additive grammars, these multiplicative calculii.

Thus, in both of these pacific and exaggerating endeavors, there is most evident the noun verb object relationship which, at least within experience and, in fact, in our thinking, we would rather know, we would prefer to experience, as a noun verb noun experience, with the understanding that we are, after all and at our best within these experiences, equatable, capable of pure identities in identification with that inseparable, but other, identity. It is, actually, the subtraction, and most certainly not the subjection, of the object, which makes for us of these endeavors the articulate sphere of our articulating experience, which makes us prefer the imagined future to an imagined past, and the present to either. It is within our understanding of the necessary contagions, no fault of their own, of these experiences, that we recognize with our and its own force, the self-valuations of living as one.

These series of invigorating endeavors must function, if they are to function, to invigorate their users with the pleasant nausea of deinhibitionizations, these being the graphic facets whereby they continue. Thus, whether we have imagined ourselves in their prodution or their use, and as we find that in producing we are users and in using, producers, we are shuttled within the subtle containers of frames and of movements into the already addicted and blatantly contagious region of anaphoras. The sequences of frames reproduce themselves only slightly less regularly in the periodic uses of our attentions to them, and the sequences of sexual movements move us no less regularly to repeat them. It is the phrase of the evening that is so commonly begun with the one, and the phrase of sleep even more commonly with the other. As we habituate ourselves as the users of these mediums, and as the mediums of their use, we notice ourselves in the pleasures of their regularity, and within the casual insistence of this regularity we regularly reproduce them. It would require, for any one of us, perhaps more than a logarithm to positively identify this regularity as an image, but within our lives, which are in one sense nothing more than the matrix of such imaginable logarithms, we recognize them, producing and reproducing them that they might have for us some space. And they are among those rare spaces which negate nothing, which explains our willing participation in these activities which are, after all, not compulsory. We are so touched in our use of these, that our actions in them are occasioned by those nervous palpitations and fluctuations which are internal to life and which control it, very much like that one which opens and closes for us our eyelids, an action which, by the way, would seem to be a minor one only if we failed to recognize that it permits to use those visual sensations so implicitly necessary to, and occasioned by, our indulgences with those activities with which we are only temporarily more concerned.

Various distinctions emit themselves in the vicinity of these vicinities, which we have divided for the furtherance of pleasures, and which occasionally, as now, we combine for the furtherance of pleasures. Drawing vertical, temporary, and unnecessary limits within the horizon of times, we must admit that: person seduces person, person touches person, persons fuck, persons separate, person leaves person, and, within the syntax of our understanding of film, wherein we make for our understanding and for our pleasure more explicit distinctions, maker makes film, maker releases film, viewer views film, viewer releases film. Without negating their differences there is inscribed at the center of these two activities which, only for our convenience we have inscribed as capable of centers, a still point, whether of fucking or of viewing, which functions as the flexing hinge upon which their neighboring verbs ride, towards which they come, in order to, and which they leave, in order to be more expressively one that will come again. And this hinge is not, actually, a thing but, rather, it is the recurrent fact which permits its surrounding functions to make of it the product of those functions, to make us productive of them and which, finally and with eloquent force, makes of these functions the objects of our recognitions, and whereby we recognize our more fully elaborated selves. This is, at base, the meaning of nouns and of verbs, that in the simple movement of noun verbing noun we recognize no triangulation, no duplicity but, casually, an identity. It is this identity, and within this equation, that both love and art, each of which is nothing more than the experience of this acting identity, and each of which is recognized, in the world, as its recognition, it is this which we live in order to experience, and in each of which we attempt that description of each which is so excellently incapable of words. It is one pecularity of the language of our culture which will not permit us to express this most basic of things as the life-making identity which it is, and which, rather forces us to express it as the relationship, the relationships, which we have become accustomed to making, in our minds, of it. It is our minds of which we must more excellently make the hinge of our experience such that we may live there what elsewhere we cannot excellently express, but which we live everywhere and always if thus we think. It is no wonder that we experience as rapture that which we cannot express, and it is no wonder that we would continue to experience as rapture that which, could we express it, would remain among the rare instances of the indivisible within our lives. Perhaps it is the inexpressibility of this relationship which makes of it for us, the verdict of our lives.

Noun verbs noun. Within the intractability of this equation without sides, the latter of these nouns verbs also, and equally, the former, and it is this that makes for us that inexpressibility which we experience as perfection, and which constitutes, for us, the possibility of a definition of perfection. The difficulty is then, in the necessity for the verb and for our difficulty in experiencing it as proceeding in each direction at once, and we would not wish to have to separate these inseparable directions. The object of these differences exists nowhere in the verbs, and nowhere in the nouns, except that one of these nouns is separated, by us, from the other, such that we perceive, think, and make, an object. It is so much too simple a thing, that we have for two identifiable things two separable words and that we make of that which, in precious experiences we identify, a division which is necessary only to, and through, our language. This separation of two things which are inseparable in those experiences which we now elucidate, is that which brings before us their inseparability, and which makes for us of the experiences of their inseparability the absolute valuation of living them. They are intransitive and it is the intransitive which yields us to our selves, which retains for the noun the absolute plausibility of the noun, without extension. It is in this way, and only within this way, that we, as individual identities, understand our selves, those peculiarities which only peculiarly divide themselves, and which only of necessity unite.

Noun verb noun. Noun verbs noun. But these are columns which never speak. They are a triangulation which merely catches the light, in order to express it. These are the three words on the screen. These are the three words in bed. In other words these three words deport themselves at various ingles, with various results, and with unvarying insistence.

What is it that these words express that doesn't enter words.
These three words are all nouns when we think about them.
These three words are all verbs when we are alive. And it is
living which teaches us that we do not need them. This fashions
the problem. In filming and in sex this problem, the problem
of arbitrary triangulations, is the problem which forms life.
And it is art which solves, no, which obliterates, this problem,
in directing the triangle to be a line. That is its activity and
that is its strength, and it is the straightening of those angles
which makes of sex the coupling line of sight. It is in this sense
in which these coupling grammars occur outside of them-
selves. If you relax all of your senses you live this straightening
of the angles, the angle. This triangulation ends in the simplicity
of perception, the solemnity of the viewing room, the laughter
of the bed, the laughter of the viewing room, the solemnity
of the bed. Thus, the line, of sight which lives life.

We will never be done with speaking of the noun verb noun of
those two specialized and specializing functions, which are
special at least in that they do remain so while we live, but
when we step outside even momentarily, certain volumes of
adjective and of adverb accrue among them, drawn there,
whether by, or to, and these small sequestering creatures of
sensations daunt these functions, such that they stagger, and
into a bliss that is momentary, and out of a bliss that lasts.
For these various special, very accurate, and very solid relation-
ships, are subject to the small viruses of an overloaded attention
which too many of us bequeath to too much of our lives.
And these small fractions of perception, which when they
do attach themselves to functions, become temporary fractions
of those functions, themselves specialize. The adjective, we
know, specializes in the noun, the adverb, upon the verb.
But there is more to it than that. And, speaking again and
simply, we would say that the adjective specializes in what
we must not for long know about each other, about each
thing, that the adverb specializes in what we must not, for long,
be knowing of each action, each sequence moving. These small
flourishes which blemish when they do utter, do so because

each more specializes that more simple function, because each
expresses more the bequeathed and lingering artifacts of other
lives, other voices, other thought. Person fucks person. This
person is me. Person makes film, person views film. This person
is me. But. Adjective person fucks adjective person. But. Person
adverb fucks person. But. Adjective person makes adjective
film, person adverb makes film. This person is me only when
especially me. Otherwise, I am the reader, the viewer, the
voyeur, in either case excluded, by adjectives, by adverbs.
In other words, adjectives and adverbs measure distances,
just as tempos and punctuations measure times. In other words,
adjectives and adverbs measure our distances, from our lives.
Adjectives can only describe for us, and especially if we spec-
ialize in thinking about it, the lives we would not wish to lead,
and adverbs can describe for us only those times we would
not wish to have, those times in which we could not live. It
is true that these small things do enliven the grammars of these
acts, our actions, but they are a special glamor with which we
adorn our ·lives, not in order to live them but within that
rather lazy gesture whereby we try to make them special.
And so it is natural that they fail us, within distance and in
time, that it is they which cause us to fail. It is they which
will cause us to die, and more frequently to forget, for we
burnish these simple and factual actions, of death and of for-
getting, which we call, perhaps, morbid, and so die, which we
call, perhaps, failure, and so lose in forgetting. And it is by
them that these things that we are discussing, filming and
fucking, and which we would want to last, would die. We must
not indulge with other than their own simplicity those things
which are simple, or we do not simply fuck, we do not simply
watch, we do not simply make. Instead, we would be making
of something which would simply make us live, something
which will simply make us die. It is the triumph of these small
particles which adhere to us that we cannot easily ignore
them, and it is our own triumph when we do.

The connectives of grammar modify, they tinge, all of dis-
course, all of thought, but with vagueness. The dark line

between the individual frames of film, the breaths of sex, tinge life with its own faintness, its character, its depth. These lines between and among the mounting equations of viewing and of passion, are the interludes that make possible times. Connections separate, and in this separation is the permissions for failures, that permission which demands failure plans it, breaks it, and brings it about. These are the conjunctions, the asides of punctuation, the ampersands, the prepositions, and the clauses. These are those interiors within the interiors we inhabit, within those in which we live, these are the bracketed and bracketing interiors of choices, mistakes, losses, withdrawals, and death. In the clear spaces of insistent passing actions there are no connections, only the arbitrary breath, and the arbitrary gaze, the beautiful absent sex which inhabits two lives, and the beautifully absent sight, which motivates two lives. The maker makes and the viewer takes. The viewer makes a little too. The lover loves and the loved one takes. The loved one makes a little, too. These triumvirates in action stabilize the worlds of our lives, but, within each connection they falter, bury their action, stop their life, and die. Only the ongoing plunge of fascination lives, and it is not connected. Only life goes on, and it is the equilateral distance from each of its instances, whereby it goes on, whereby noun verbs noun, whereby maker makes, something, whereby viewer views, something, whereby fucker fucks, someone, whereby someone fucks, someone. Such that even the object becomes a questionable stance of the pursuit, something which the subject appears to demand, and only appears, to demand, for the furthering satisfaction of the subject, of subjects. But only the overly literate demands the connections. Even the illiterate demands the object. The grammar of sex is the grammar of film, and the grammar of film is the grammar of sex, but without connections, without embellishing words, without any interferences from time or the trapped and trapping notions of space, that is, purely, without regret. In the living space of our lives, adjectives make nouns sick, adverbs stop words, make them dead, and the small connections make life small, trapping the integers in a sequence they neither demand nor deserve. Nouns are alive. Verbs know they are alive. Objects are, though they need not be, the representation of the choice of nouns. These three simple, and latter, things, are the substance of our adequate knowledge of the world, and the necessity of our life within it.

The living versions of truth are lodged, in a language, in the nouns and verbs, not as such but as they relate, as they live, moving one another in the actions of desire, in which they live and make life, or in those other actions wherein they stop. It is the lived versions of accuracy which, and aside from this, inhabit the adjective and the noun, and it is these versions whereby they approach, or cover, our lives. It is the so-called minor parts of speech which, when we live them, angle into our lives at angles of acute or obtuse direction, that is, at angles either slightly or greatly aberrant from that direction of our living. On the other hand, when a noun pursues a noun through an action which a verb aligns, the direction is thus far clear, direct, and simple. It requires that humility characteristic of courage, and that courage character-istic of humility, to accept this, and to live it. We are herein talking about living in the relationships of film, and of sex, in order to make this more apparent, in order to be able to say, with a conviction and from inside of our life, that we do not need to live outside of it, in those things which language touch-ing life merely affixes to it, and that in proceeding with those open motions characteristic of film, whereby its movement from reel to reel passes that juncture with light in order to come on the screen, or that in proceeding with the open motions characteristic of sex, whereby the movements from person to person pass that nervous junction of passions in order to come, that it is here, and precisely here, that we live without knowing it, without needing to know it, and without wanting to. And so herein we recognize the necessity of focus to these acts, unfettered and unbound, but willful, or desiring, of that absolute attention which gratifies, boundless, finally, but in that one direction which alone succeeds for desires, bringing to them, and bringing them to, that point from which nothing is absent, to which nothing is added, screwing us firmly to our seats, lighting us when we come, such that the focus of our lives in mind is for those moments complete, absolute, and powerful with those powers whereby we do go on, to live, and to do it again. This focus is a focus which we bring, of necessity to these acts, and in order that they act, and this focus is a focus they return to us, and in order that we act. This focus is then, nothing other than, and not apart from, that absolutely linear directness of pursuit of noun by noun in verb. Within the constraints of the world, whose constraints are its modifiers, its modification, this focus is difficult and, overcoming that difficulty, coming through it, we experience that ecstasy whereby we recognize it, wherein we know ourselves in knowing nothing other, wherein we come, through our selves, to that unity wherein is simple action, wherein we simply act, wherein we release thoughts, to act our lives, to live our actions, to come to be.

Within the simplicities of the noun verb noun relationship there is, yet, room for some complexity, or for those subtleties which we encounter as such, those differences which are difficulties only if we think about them and which, otherwise, disclose themselves to us as things which act, or as actions moving things. One such complexity is a duplicity in the language thought gives to films, in contrast to a unity parallel to it in the language thought gives to sex. Maker makes film. Viewer views film. Person fucks person. This might be explained simply, of course, by the existence of film as something outside of persons which, then, by extension, is something different to that person who makes it and to that person who views it. Or if we ascribe more recognizably proper nouns to the sexual act we recognize the ascription to it of a relationship closer to that which we have just recognized in our donation of language to film. Joe fucks Sarah. Sarah fucks Joe. We have now, in statements in which language sixty-nines itself, a noun internal to each person when we separate their times, to give meaning to them separately. But this movement away from person fucks person is precisely that movement which, particularly if it stops to articulate itself within the fact of the act, alters the singular unity of that act whereby it translates for us as ecstacy. We might also view this difference between film and sex as consequent of the duplicity of verbs within the language thought gives to film, in that we recognize within that sphere a making and then a viewing, and we might then posit the existence of the doubled nouns in relation to these verbs as consequent of their plurality, whereby we would be saying that differing actions require, whether for their actors or for what is acted upon, an equally differing set of nouns. But this nominal difference occurs only within the subjective portion of the language, and not within the objective sphere where film remains standard as the object of both making and viewing. In other words, we recognize in film an object which extends through two different verbs to two different subjects. We recognize in sex a verb which extends in one direction, twice, to a subject and an object which, if not identical, appear to mirror each other adequately, producing those consequences of that unity which we have been discussing. Or we might, if we wished, and moving only slightly from what we have just said, say that the verb in the sexual relationship moves, not twice in one direction, but once in two. In either event we are left, in our understanding of language's use of these relationships, with a relationship in film which is hinged at the object, and with a relationship in sex which lies flat about the verb. Accepting the simplicity of this, and the greater accuracy of language in relation to those things which are simple, which it has perhaps recognized first and in relation to which it has then had longer to perfect itself, we confront again, but hopefully in greater clarity, that specialization of the language depictive of differences which we had recognized at once. We must now explain those pleasures we make, and take, within these differing modes, or within these modes wherein we make perhaps a mistake in recognizing difference, in separating, at all, an action from itself.

If film divides itself away from its object, it is in order to

seek, through its verbs, those subjects which it might thereby
inhabit. And if sex settles itself about its verb, it is in order
to equalize its subjects, and its, and their, various objects,
of attention, of intention. Such that we are given in this that
which each is, film an object in search, through means, of
subjects, and sex a verb, seeking in subjects, between subjects,
and in objects, between objects, that most splendid, and that
most simple, accord. It is the singularity of the verb of sex
wherein we recognize that unity, and whereby we must recog-
nize in it the base of all basic unity, even that of film. And
it is in the duplicity within the actions of film, in its seeking
through doubling verbs, doubling subjects, that we recognize
its hierarchization of life, of lives, whereby we know that
we can, with the permission of its verbs, live in it. For it is
nouns as subjects and as objects which are the substances
of hierarchies, and it is verbs which are the flat movers of life.
Nouns separate themselves in space, and verbs flatten them-
selves in time. It is we who, as living nouns, contract these, as
obstacles, into some attempts at understanding of such as sex,
and of film. The nouns sequester themselves in order to perfect
themselves as nouns, in order to be nouns, and the verbs draw
the nouns to the nouns, in order to be functional verbs. Again,
in this, we recognize the primacy of the verb, such that we go
home again, from the divided selves of film, to the self of
sex, from that illusion which we willingly grant to film of
some form of permissive identity in and to it, to the demands
of sex, which are for unity, and only within it. Or, to put
this simply, film permits a unity which sex completes, or,
art offers us those versions of that unity which we complete
in life. The nouns of film live two at a time, one living
through what it has made, for itself and for others, and one
living through what has been made, for it, and for and by
that other. The nouns of sex live one at a time, or, that is
to say, as two, or as several, at once, within the unity of a verb
which were it to serve as metaphor for film would fall apart,
there, about the two, or several, nouns, subjects to objects,
and objects of subjects. But these separated actions, of film
and of sex, do not remain always as separate as at base they

seem, and are. Each moves, at times, film through its approach to excellence, and sex, through its coloration by adjectives or adverbs, in what we might then call the direction of what we might then call, the other. And it is about this notion of the other wherein exists those divisions which we make, that film involves that veritable contagion of others about an object, that sex involves the contagion of its verb between those which, otherwise, would be others, that film is, then, a passion for discourse, and sex a passion for intercourse, that motion which, as sex, is the most silent of languages, the widest, and the strongest. It is, but only to the largest extent, art whereby we direct a life, and sex whereby it is directed. It is nouns wherein we recognize a life, and verbs wherein it is inflected. Or, and to be more blunt about it, it is in other nouns and when we recognize therein a life, that we recognize in us that life, and it is in verbs, and verbs alone, that life lives life, and us. But we will not for long separate these things, if we live, and we will continue to live if we live only within that unity whereby life verbs life, and wherein that unity lives as, is, a verb.

Film has historically followed a line from black and white to color, if we call that a line, and as we caution ourselves in making those distinctions. Sex, but only frequently, follows that direction from lights and colors to dark, or darkened spaces, from eyes wide open to eyes shut, or periodically shutting. Thus film has gone, though probably for purely technological reasons, from an imitation of eyes more flatly, or more obliquely, sensitive, than ours, through a fairly good approximation in two dimensions of our own ability, and inability, to see, and in some specific cases has, in the visual sphere taken separately, given us not simply what we would not otherwise see but also what we would not otherwise be able to see, and has thereby, and within narrowing cases, given us the abilities to go on seeing as such, with heightened abilities. The movement has been, within its best instances, what we might call the verticalization of our sense of sight, raising it from the relatively flat tonality permitted on the plane of ocular experiences habitable as shades of black and white, through an approximation of that dimensionality which we experience in and as color, to the almost total verticalization inhabited by what we might now be calling art films, wherein the object, film, moves vertically through the space of the eyes, rather than the eyes through it. Sex, of course, habitually involves a heightening of the senses about the dimensions, and a heightening through the totality of the body, of bodies, of those dimensions as experienced as such, but sex is of course also a specialist in the vertical, it specializes the body in the direction of its weightless verticalization, an experience of the body's absence within an experience of the total presencing of the body, such that, and especially toward the climaxing of sexual acts, color matters little and more frequently not at all, and blackness is attained, perhaps metaphorically, as that colorless dimension in which the body achieves its pleasures. The pleasure of the eyes is a heightening of the presence of the bodies, and the pleasure of the body is a relaxation of the presence of the eyes.

As we strengthen our physical stride, as we lengthen our mental stride, in pursuit of these elusive facets of our lives, elusive because so very present, we arrive first at sex, then at film. These studies, whether through walking or in thinking, are a version of the verb to live, and we live first through our bodies, and later, though equally, through our minds. We arrive first at the verbs of sex, because we arrive via verbs, and secondly at the objects of film, because objects are what we arrive at. If by verbs we arrive, we arrive in not stopping, and if at objects we arrive, we arrive to stop, and go on therein in only the verbs within those objects. If in arriving in the verbs of sex we stop, we stop by, are stopped by, objects, and if in arriving at the objects of film we keep going, that is, if we keep arriving, we do so through the verbs, if excellent, within the objects of those bodies of light. The approach of the mind is always in the direction of the mind; the approach of the body is always in the directions of the body. These approaches are not separate, they are, in fact, inseparable, within the lives of the verb. The verb drives the film from reel to reel, the body from body to body, and the mind within the mind. The object is a blockade in the path of thought, in the projection of the reel, and in the body to which the body objects. The body comes in the bodies of consciousness, the objects of art come in the subjects attendant to the objects of art, and, in thought, the mind comes in the mind. All of the objects of attention, and those of intentions, get fucked by the verbs, and the verbs fuck with satisfaction in the advancing verbs. The cadences of the armatures of thought reach both of these locations, in verbs and in nouns, in nouns as subjects and as objects, and the locating is the verb which locates the nouns in locations. In sex the verbs capture the nouns, are the willed living of the nouns, and in films, the nouns capture the verbs of the living of the eyes, to be the willing habitation of those verbs. And this discourse is the habitation of neither samenesses nor differences. These are the spaces which times inhabit, and the times in which spaces live. The separations are a convenience of thought, and thought is the convenience of separations, so fuck that, and look at that.

If topology were the place the word came from,

nouns would stand horizontal, verbs stiff and vertical in vertically falling reason.

The confidence of the work, its competence, is then, its having been *there.*

Every word is our word, each pollution.
The plethora of gesture, not even understood as such, pollutes.
Theorized writing clears, non-programmatically, the controllable soft air, the air of durable words.

A more disturbable appearance is apparent if the time of the place changes underneath the word, arguing without proof that its feet've moved.

Have this language for which to in; there is no thing other with which to decorate it, no other reply. "Echo is the nominal origin of echo (verbal)," this being something we say only much later, 'later' defined as a little prior to our definition of this latter word.

The work exists to end in a world.
This demands de-pollutive character of all work, which must gratify the necessity, justify position, in the garbage state of language.

The world is simply this plenitude. The language is simply that plenitude.

The notion *that words come out of the mouth is counterproductive. It makes people do it.*
Language gets all thrown into the world; instead, of being made (to be) or there.

Language bores the words.
Either these two weights are waited for or then lost.
Language bores the world.

Fortunately the hand is slow and can be further stilled.

A radial attentiveness can shut up the world.

I.e. i.e.

Speech is relatively durable, language a dry solid waste.

Speaking:—the tragic form of thought.

Language is unclear. The apparent loss is (the apparence loss is is. . .) gain in thought. Thought speaks as listening.

It all loses time from the imaginary present, a (sic) past (sic), such that.

Language is a permeable substance founded on the thinking thinking's in. The thinking mind hasn't reasons.

In language, in writing, we remember our losing, exact our sequence. Actuality complete.

Thinking is its own literature, perseverant. Literature, a bad faith thought endures. Speech dies.

A fear of speaking as I think a ballet of illusions. Let the work turn itself. I made it with my hammer.

Language is disabused by thought. Thought's, ponderous. Language gently seeks accord in, with, thought. It utters itself perfectly to be thinking.

In an angle between thought and memory: language. Or a rapid desire to be being there. Or a vapid desire to be being there. I have my own future in forgetting. In each excusing absence, a word (f̶o̶r̶) being there.

Language is not a virus. Wm is wrong. Speech is viral over recalcitrant thought, the body which appears us, (as), language.

ZEN?   WHO KNOWS?

or
A Small Statement of Disbelief for Norman Fischer

What doesn't signify? Walking down the street you might see
red hair passing. At that moment of recognition, the red hair is
a signifier, signifying its signified, the word *red*.

There is nothing arbitrary about the sign. When we think that
there is we are noticing our own confusion about the arbitrary
way, and our own arbitrariness about the confusing way, in
which we have assigned it to a place or to places in our mind, in
our uses of it, in the world, and so on.

In fact, what is interesting, is the act of recognition.
*

The zen master says to you: "When sitting, just sit." Then, as
if not wanting you to be bored, he gives you a koan upon
which to concentrate as you sit. Perhaps we have learned to
delineate: When sitting, just sit; when doing koan, just do
koan; when sitting and working on koan, just sit and work on
koan.

I would not try to define koan practice. And yet to say what I
would say, that koan practice is its own definition, is already
also my definition of it. In fact, just: koan practice.

But I will admit that as I understood and used koan practice
at one time, it was that very solipsistic nature of it, or which
I ascribed to it, which perhaps was that about it which most
appealed to me. This solipsism, which I would define by refer-
ring to its tautological tendencies, was at that time congruent
with, or at least in metonymic accord with, other circular

tendencies of thought, feeling, action, and the circulating tendency to separate them. This is something which I think we all understand. We all live, were educated, and think, in the so-called west, in western ways. We have all shared in the production of oppositions, definitions, delineations, and dialectics.

Perhaps we have all done too much without having done enough. Perhaps we have all made the mistake of doing that, of thinking that, of calling that a mistake, and so on.

*

What is the relationship between koan study and writing?

Neither of them can be described, neither of them makes any sense, and maybe we should leave it at that.

One can talk about them, but *describe* them? and be done with it? And the longer they're talked about, the less sense either makes, or is it, perhaps, that the more sense either makes the less necessity is attached to the doing of either? Let's do one or the other, or both, and a few other things too, and, yes, leave them all at that.

Zen. Who knows?

*

It is frequently asserted that discovery is a process of redefinition, and frequently it is explained that growth also is a matter of redefining values and the like. But seldom is this understood, and more seldom yet for what it really is.

First, it is important to leave the definitions alone. They're too sluggish for words. If we must imagine it this way at all, think of the dictionary page, then, leave the definitions alone and move the words around. In this way, courage is attainable, for instance, rigor will achieve a new value, simplicity will get its due, and an alert life of pleasure will be possible. These are examples from my experience. You know what you need.

And last, we might do well to leave the definitions, as they say, behind. Entirely behind.

ESSAI A CLEF

Mr. Barthes, having written his own image into a text (*Barthes by Barthes*) and the chief of his obsessions into another (*A Lover's Discourse*), died. This latter text, death a life among *dead* letters, leaves to us the task of pursuit, the cherishing of his mind's image in his mind's words.

It is enough to say that this magazine owes its existence or if not, the meaning of that existence, to the significant desire-producing language mechanisms which Mr. Barthes constantly refurnished with his analyses of/as text.

*

It is his contribution, initialled by his perseverance, to discern that it is a failure of critical writing to view its task as the reading of a text; excellent critical, *attentive*, writing knows its task to be the reading of the *writing* of a text.

Barthes' analyses of prose literature, in moving from writing to text as object, observed a regalvanization of literary effort. He observed in the stylization of thought into writing, paradigms for the constructs of all carriers of meaning. His distillative attention to these modes enriched the scope of a mind's attentiveness to itself: in the details of thought's passing into signed meaning, the world. The effervescence of literary writing is function of the sign's interest in itself. Nothing is ever more absent from excellent writing than its writer. Indeed, this "its writer" evaporates facing the sign of a question. It need not be; any text demands its own insouciant definition about it in the world, its satisfaction.

The text stands each word on its end, drops it and draws it back, propels it vertically and regains it. This plunging and striving, an activation at rest, performs before the world its calling into question and the at once clean maculate articulation texting its response: text, a one sided call and echo. This plummet, this rise, is thought; the text is its activation, its notice. Form is the mode for thought, language its inseparable substance; the text a manipulation of form through language. Life is the substance of language.

((Unless it be one, the poem is a very small thing in this world of text. Now that we understand ourselves as we write, we can think.))

*

Roland Barthes isolated from among the many symptoms of language its being-as-symptom, its signification. Language is structure. Structure, later, constitutes its materialization as text. The language, a blank egoless object bordering on operation, finds in its egos-recipient (readers) what it deposits; at best, i.e. in text, this deposit is structure, deposit void of all but the gesture of deposition. The mind creates of every meaning the sign of itself; but within this operation the author need not be ego-producer; this is the meaning of text: that *structure* produces.

Barthes: meaning is articulation.

Wittgenstein: meaning is use.

The text is the meaning-quotient of language; each text measures again its meaning-value in structuration. The text isolates space between the lived elements of life in order to be itself recognized; it does this by thinking, by structuring. The textual structuration occurs always equidistant from the sets of its possible choices and the pursuit through those sets; it poses always a horizon, the image of difficulty by which it is recognized.

((A writer may aim to produce "private property language."))

((Writing produces, and is concerned with producing, exceptions to the notion that its model is speech.))

((An effort of writing is to alter the language such that speaking it has value. Writing offers the possibility of reproportioning the volumes of language and speech.))

((Writing distributes simultaneously the function of each of its elements.))

((The larger the unit of language, the greater the combinatory freedom. Thus, e.g., prose promulgates attitude.))

*

Roland Barthes attended the prevalence of the sign as meaning-carrier; his attentions isolated the significant.

Meaning and concept combine as/under the aegis of sign. This sign stands in the world as form, subsequently combining with concept, in creating and maintaining the entire realm of signification.

*

Text reads (me).

Texts read.

As critic: into the excipient body of the text the alert mind inscribes what it has been the text's to inscribe in the excipient mind. This gesture of mirroring mimes one of replacement. Each signifier becomes something of a shifter; shifters are tautological, they speak/write themselves, delivered *and* mirrored.

Reading acts text.

Each text rereads (me); recalls remembering.

The language is, its operations are, the go-between (shifting mechanism) in this function of trade, reader exchanged for text and text for reader; this exchange of valuing is signified by the reader's return to the text and by the text's return to the reader in memory; it is a paratactic contract, twice signed for.

As the text's various signifyings leap variously and repeatedly out of it (under a duress of reading), it assumes a personality; it is this alternate with which the reader exchanges thought, as the text reinforces him/her to think. It is signifiers which the reading tends to distill, to make of the act a meaning indivisible. As part of this formulating, the reader, employing reading, interrogates the text in order to be him/herself disclosed; this is an action to seek the bounds of the textual enclosure, the limited world. The reader unites what the writer has used languages to hold apart; he/she remembers what the writer was

interested in forgetting, losing, loosing (to begin to think to
write is to remember, to write is to forget). The meaning is the
aura of the reading, a calculated advance on further reading
which draws the reader on. Reading and writing advance,
equally, the text; the reader subjects the text to this further-
ance.

The text is consumed greedily, because its failures are
enticing. The text is an agglomeration, read as a map, of failed
exigencies; it is the sum of traces of impurities; it is these which
the writer of a text tends to forget from the language, as he
writes. The reader disturbs the text by his/her interest, even as
it is being written. In fact, the text is the reader's product,
matrices of meanings which he/she releases as product from
the significations of the writing, which has been the author's
product. The text, by its inclusiveness, attempts to choke the
reader, so that he/she utter no *sound* of his/her own; it is an
ecological effort, which the reader in part maintains as in
reading he/she confronts, disturbs, distributes, the text's
intentional unity. This is an allure of the text, that it is in
reading disturbed but not damaged, that it disturbs without
damage; a faultless assurance of furthered interest, upon
which, manifested, the reader capitalizes; the mutual debt of
reader and author is disturbed by the text, which advances
to the reader a material interest it had not in writing for the
author (hence an author's obsession with like texts). It is the
text, synchronically a social mien/mean, which writes its
unity, a dimension shared, barely but totally, by author and
reader, at an edge of their activity. This is the text's economy;
though it is full, its effects are not displaced even by the
coterminous attentions of reader and author. Even their calling
it names, leaves it still. But the text is not closed; it inscribes
an ideal social syntax, one without waste in relations, capable
of uniting persons who it writes face to face at its one side;
entering it, leaving it, no problem.

Text texts text.

*

The text, puritanical in scope, within bounds, is not so
in essence. It is along the acultural, desiring edge of language

that the text is written; its other edge, a boundary synchronous with usage, merely supports, permits it. The competition between the two edges, a contest which the vertical of desire always champions, nevertheless furthers within the text an apprehension of its dissolve; it is against this latter uncertainty that the text finally closes, a wheel in motion which apparently stops, reverses, in having sped out of one perceptive possibility on entering another (writing, to text, say; or, text to apprehension). In separating us from usage-language, the text creates in us a great desiring for same, which it satisfies completely but in quite another way, offering in a cleansed language occasion the superlative of our own actual gestures in desiring. It seduces, in part, by exploiting a flaw, an opening, in us, the separateness of our two languages (daily; textual) with which we meet the occasion of seeking a perfection in the latter. The text loses us, forgets us, from social language. Drawing us, as itself, out of the body of that language, we lose ego, we die happy.

The author through the text demands pleasure for the reader. He/she abolishes a consumption of literature by filling its vacancy with bliss. The reader completes for moments the text's desiring motions, a completion instantly reawakening, unsatisfied, demanding after this one furtherance, another of the language. The text gives rise in the reader to one fear, that of its dissolution, which would deny to the reader his/her own anticipated dissolve into pleasure; this latter the text cannot deny, it must keep its promise excellently. The text's economy is guaranteed by the demands which must be met at its conclusion, a point, a vista to which it comes. The text permits a sort of necrophiliac pleasure: the desserts of the dead, or at least constrained, social language are enjoyed in the instance of the burgeoning textual assault, an erection of exacting consequence in a relative void of diversions and difficulties. Enjoying the corpsing of a language, suddenly puritanical ourselves, we are somewhat repelled by the image the text supplies of ourselves abandoned in such pleasure (we giggle); against this social difficulty, the text offers its pleasure, a hierarchy cleansed of social burden, a gesture completely filling a gesture. This is the text's obscenity, that, like any other, it posits itself as a substitute for discourse, it excerpts itself from the political except as a superlative instance of its negative, a diligence of pleasure escaped from its toil.

*

The text comes from its industry.

The text is trivial only in its affectations, that it appears to be literature.

The text considers its veils its triumph: an illusion.

The text does not stop to *consider* its edges.

If there were a diametrics of the text it would be one-sided, written.

The text is an animated perfection. If it fail in either of these it is, obviously, merely animated, merely perfect. Merely *split*.

Poems have dripped into the text. It is full of them.

Context, no such thing.

The convention of language is discarded for its invention.

The text durates. This is its relation with time.

The text is sentenced to reality, it is a contiguous figment, an act in an act.

The text repeats and tells.

The text is language raised to a third power: it is the (1) inhabited (2) space of a (3) builder.

The text, unlike its mention, is not historical; it does not disagree with itself. But it is an authority upon its occasion. The text exists of several diachronic scenes at once.

The text sits on itself, excreting the text. It takes literature apart, to be. The writing of the text is an operation on successive operations.

The text binds time to a contract. It does this instant by instant. But time forgets.

The text is written along a vector between intellect (makes new) and intelligence (remembers).

The text satisfies by more than it was made to produce, in spite of its consistent language.

The text consumes an oedipal image in order to play with

itself without bother.

In each text the language is decided a unit of space. This makes it complete.

The text is elaborate because it enforces an attitude. Obviously the author function is not dead.

The text is a collective; it delights.

The text may be the last act of a body. Language will act alone.

*

The life is a text. The text is a life. Life, text, are equal. The life, the text, cut equally from the world, and equally, as one, are left. Each fiction dominates only in its own territory, "succeeding" in excluding the rest. For the reader of a text, that text is all that he/she knows to be the case, but the author knows also that knowing, and a magnitude of wider bounds that that implies; in this the author and critic share, that they look at the text as, and not only through, it.

The life is a depository for thought, as the text is thought's writing. Life and the text disintegrate for time. The life, the text: each revises, but by going on, never as an afterthought, never in reverse. In the author's case, text, life, are alternate words for that one thing which each seeks to inscribe. The desire of each for the other is intransitive; each merely acts, this acting is single, unadjectivised, unextended.

The body, its life, is made evident only through language (modification); language is evidenced only in the collection of bodies, language is inherently pluralized.

Barthes' own text is a figment of fragments: he took his life apart, and kept it there. Definitions he manipulated re-appear: the figment is of continuity. A flatness is required of the fragments, or of their field of signifieds, in order to overcome any illusion about them: an *admission* of flatness. For this, a structure without systems is required. A collection of utterances become any life: against this, for the author a text is a remission from life, a forgetting-machine.

Each text is an appropriation from the language. This separates the author from it also. Time is consumed because/ where there is not enough of it. There are enough texts (undemanded); this sufficiency paradoxically guarantees against consumption. The text is in need of a pronoun of its own.

((Theory is *essentially* heavy; bears at once the preponderance of an at least two-sided utterance; speculates at least in two directions, that of its "object" and that of itself.))

((To disintegrate (language) *actively*, *is* revolution. The contraentropic is entropy speeded up.))

((Connotation is a matter of existence.))

((Style: the rubric which is visible *through* the work.))

((Sentences, singly, are impotent (the maxim comes in its own mouth); together, they perform texted orgiastic gesture.))

((Aesthetic gesture may meet the ideological at a point in the mind when it is *grasped*, understood. Ideological discourse never reaches the aesthetic because it does only one thing, its open mouth.))

((The image-system, an attended-to and delineated symbol: of ego.))

((Antithesis *deserts* language in a futile effort to become ideological.))

((Aesthetic language is ironic; we are amused/taken by its self-absorption.))

   *

Signification is a function of history. It is a paradox that history, the deadest of languages, speaks. Nothing leads us to expect this mis-giving away of material, certainly not the text, whose elucidation of the same material is transparent by comparison. Perhaps history too will stop speaking, to be text.

There is a fluctuant, ahistoric zone between our need to utter and the guise (writing) whereby we occasionally solve for that need. The text is an extreme of utterance close to that zone, taking from that zone a veiled ardor, giving to it what little definition it has. In this zone the signifier is loosed, disobliged, given to be given, taken apart, among signifiers alone, untaxed.

History is the landscape of textual activity: i.e. the text bears historical traces, but these traces are free within the text to bear precisely and only themselves, unconstrained, a mirror against a mirror. And it is this latter lack of distance, this infra-closeness, which permits the tranversed but undivided text, the texting of histories, a superlative of geometic progresses. The text is active twice-at-once, bringing to itself dispersed particular signifiers, and releasing them as one material: a plural, but singularizing, activity: meaning.

On the plane of signification, however, each signifier is entirely separate, secluded. Needs motivate a combination of such as recognition, memory, mental industry, which enforce the various plural presencings of signifiers, a sort of failure of them, a letting down. The attenuations are marvelous.

(History is much shorter than the text, one signifier among many. The text is much shorter than history, one occurrence among many.) The text exhausts history.

*

It is in peregrinations, mental or otherwise, of lover pursuing beloved, that love resembles the warp and woof of textual fabrication. In a beloved, in the text, an image is sought of an ineffable moment, a vertical duration within unhalting horizontal passage.

Adjectives merely circulate in the effort to define the affairs of love or the text. That is to say, the notions of designation, of meaning, are subject to a furor, subject to that which animates, desire.

But to multiply such comparisons, such accords, between love and text, is to damage the completeness of the surfaces of these two subjects-as-objects, a completeness made boundless by the play of superlatives inhabiting either (overlapping) sphere. But the love-text? it would require two writing-subjects, not synonymous, but coterminous: a figure available as a delicacy in the text, but difficult of apprehension in the world.

In order to remain outside my subject, *I* speak, and within this suddenly magnified spectacle (a world!) I stop to write.

PLANISHING HAMMER

Organized language is a trace of effort. The solidity of the lines is trust; we rest *in* our work, *whatever* comes out of the heterogeneous world formulating into this graspable world, because the structure divides it for us.

The language is fragment. It is only a fearful mind that sees this as disintegration. This cutting is the very sign of unity, of solid excitement, the sign of structure. The manipulation of units of language in durable structures, is literature. Though they may be interesting singly, only structure *justifies* its fragments. The flaking arrangement of lines, of words within lines, and of line groups, convinces us that they engage each other; they are made sentient. Language cut openly bleeds meaning and thus does more than it was supposed (thought) to have done: its extension.

Each line inflects a gesture. It hurts surrounding lines, entices them, throws them, hurries them. In this writing the gestural line is never still, negative.

When lyric and imagistic modes are extended and intercut, the calculations appear at each refining turn to be reaching for conclusions. This reaching is held steady in their constant incompletion. The mastery of some formulation is implied in the turn to and from each line because that formulation is present there in it. The *forestalling* is held *repeatedly* before us; we see it as the subject. The advance implicit within each move is cancelled by its immediate repetition, but the impres-

---

This was written in response to Ray DiPalma's *Planh* which appeared in *Roof V* and *Roof VI. Planh* was republished by Casement Books, 1979.

sion of the gesture elegantly retrying itself is the substance of our impression, is our involvement.

Each stanza is three sided. This unaltered stability reinforces the line of sight we have as we progress. Our progress links the identical units. Nothing isolate, nothing diminishes. The sturdiness of the stanzas restates, as each memory reinforces others, definingly. Two gestures move together at the point of each stanza: the gesture of each stanza resting straight, the gesture of stanza after stanza undiminished by our continuing perspective. Gyroscope and metronome intersect. The two gestures are, repeatedly, one; that is the point distinguished by our presence, stanza to stanza, the persisting erection of sense.

The breaking of the poem into ten sections provides the reader ten vantage points. Like Christo's Running Fence, at each hill topped in walking we review a renewed architecture, in both directions. These horizontal and temporary though repeated experiences, of noting what has been allowed in and combined, and what excluded, fill us also vertically with the experience of disclosure; the world, the language, goes by on both sides. The stanzas are strides.

This writing is vertical not only in the sense of accumulation, from the first line to the last, but also in the sense of flight, the last line drawing (through) all others to the first. Each line is momentarily the focal point of cross currents; nothing escapes the rush. Each line is targetted, washed.

The substance of the writing is language. (Writing *elicits* the substance of writing, scrapes it together.) This is the case with works which are whole. The work, by not travelling from the domain of its tools, has only to perform itself. It is at no point separate from itself as are works which employ one device (words) for the accomplishment of another (a subject, a discourse, e.g.). Like filings held in array by a magnet, there is no separating the force from the result. The writer does not have to name himself or sign his devices, because the structure does so, for itself, self-intently. Each chunk of language is a disguised verb; it speaks itself. The words are not a display, moral or metaphysical or otherwise, they are a phenomenological fact, they can't be consumed. The substance of the writing bears upon itself, and even this only by its exclusion of the *else* which its demonstration releases from any need to be there. Our metaphors (visceral, contingent, etc.) for describing the substance, though they be accurate rhetoric, mark only our own presence and in so doing briefly relieve us of the work our presence entails.

The music of the poem is building block music. Its insistent additions make its structure more visually intuited than tonally attended. The poem sounds good without that being its intent, without the sound being gained and at the same time lost at the level of intention. Language, when it acts, works unavoidable sound. The sound *excites* the language; that is its function. The sound is a function of language's habit, something it displays as it enforces itself. The sensual phrases are not so much differentiated as arrived at; like oases, their appeal is scribed by the needs we achieve before we arrive at them. Though the sound is pleasure, the poem brings itself together not even at that slight remove which separates in our mind the sound of the hammer from the hammer. The *tools* are emphatic; not "their" "products".

The poem evidences some usual devices: rhyme, words in combination for comparison, and the results of that, insertions from the surrounding reality of a transparent writer (a persona we invent), lists of sensation or place or effect, a linear though jolting accounting for condition. But the poem is more deflected than produced by these pockets of trait and habit. We are tempted to say that the author has produced this work from his own interiors. The text provides nothing to support this idea; we must admit that we have used the most handy hypothesis, which in reality keeps us away from the poem. The poem has not produced its effects in us. We have produced the poem inseparable from its effects. Suddenly we (we the text) glance at the poem stretching about us, and see bits of our own times, particles of our own natures, laced into the eras between the lines.

The poem does not reach for an ending. This is not because of doubt. The poem contains its conclusion in each line, each measurement; retaining conclusion, it does not have to pursue it. Neither does the end connect with the beginning, though it does imply it. The poem lays over itself at *each* point. By *extension*, the poem.

From our place along its traverse, we need not speak of an end of this poem. Summary is not important; a continuing summative process is. The most pointed revelation of each line is its position. It is a marker; holds its position so cleanly that it is revealed, reveals it and so holds it. The larger meaning, that implicit in any self-supporting structure, is implicit in each reconstituted gesture; the gesture of line, of stanza, of word. There is no question of an exterior structure which we argue to intuit; words intuit, they trace, their argument is made instantly by the design they continuously perfect about them. Our gradual reading of the lines, our inspection, sees each locked firm to attention; produced by the closest reading, this is the largest meaning, the durability. We don't examine this writing against codes; it produces itself as discrete, opened code and abolished all others from purpose.

As we read line to line, each provides a pause of recognition. There is an orderly list of noticeable elements, factors. The meaning comes out of the spaces fluctuant about the lines. The lines in relation produce charges and discharges (cognition and recognition) (we are held and released), and it is this motion, this constant, that reminds us that we are in the presence of meaning. This reminder itself, unfiltered though given efflorescently from the depthed and screened filter of the words, *is* the meaning. Our implicatedness as readers completes the presence of meaning and simultaneously neutralizes it. Its presence is its vanishing, and ours.

?s to .s

for Ron Silliman and for The Chinese Notebook

3. Chesterfield, sofa, divan, couch — these are entirely different objects; they are related by the mistake we make in not having more words for more objects. They are conditions of the word 'name' used as a verb; even here we have made the same mistake.

4. It is a word every time it is used. The rest of the time.

6. Written with a different pen, it would have been a sentence. Written after with a different pen, it would have been a different sentence. Absorbed in this question, we learn that the instruments of construction have their meanings. Time is an instrument of construction.

7. It could be. A different person would make each judgement.

10. Poetry lacks surprise, form, theme, development, interest, curiosity — Always, somewhat. . . . — Never, somewhat. It is how poetry drops between these two sentences that will survive.

13. Propose the tradition, delineate it; then wait, for more of what you already have, in part, in this writing. Any proposal of the tradition is, implicitly, impact on it.

This was written in response to the questions posed in Ron Silliman's *The Chinese Notebook*, which has since been published in *The Age of Huts*, Roof, 1986.

14. Wittgenstein's contribution is *strictly* formal, but it is not only formal. He tells us about a topic, how to write for example, as Stein does. His contribution would not be strictly (sic) formal even if it were all in logical notation. *His* meditations, too.

16. If you said so.

18. Already the writing has left its Chinese notebook.

20. This is not a definition. A proposition satisfies everyone; they notice it, even unwittingly and suddenly operate with the understanding that a proposition is its means of verification.

21. There is no 'same poem'; we may only look through one text to its source, this activity then embodies a third poem, non-stop.

25. You show it in that question.

29. Ask the bird.

30. That you can imagine it answers how you can imagine it. Put the chair in a room, in an ocean, a sentence, an automobile, a thought, a word, a box.

31. A language is rational when viewed from its inside. That is part of the meaning of 'inside' in *this* grammar.

32. Languages are patricidal: there is no return from one to a former. Therapy, for instance, is designed to ease us from a held language, through (to) the choosing of another. This is one humane reason for regarding language at work.

34. Myuh gawd! I really don

35. Unpeel the onion a layer at a time; at center, the still point.

36. "SAW FIT" is the clichéic expression, use, for a structural ideal.

38. Poetry isn't more like one thing than another, though the possibility it is proposes a game. We get the clear answer to this question only as poetry's attention unremittingly locks upon itself.

39. It already is, but among so many other things that its mattering seems hardly to endure.

42. Analogies relating art forms are useful because no form contains all the languages for talking about itself.

43. "The so-called normal tongue" *is* decoration, as it is equally a fact in the world it continuously decorates.

47. We have come exactly as far as Sterne and Pope have come since Sterne and Pope.

48. The relationship between 'same' 'different' will never in writing be clear; we might think so. This question is manifest in every art.

52. Each word goes to a page of the etymologicon for its history. A hammer is driving nails, another is pulling nails, another is breaking through a wall. Use does not need history, but very seldom does it ignore history.

53. Yes, now that you have said so. Yes, now that you have said so. No, each question demonstrates its altering decision.

57. " . . . a relationship which adjectivizes is on the side of the image, on the side of domination, of death." — Barthes

58. There are. You wouldn't.

60. Categories create categories; language gets used, again, again.

61. Poetry is a state of poetry; nothing can impinge on it, though things can be thought to. That it is otherwise is believed by people outside poetry. Poetry which resists the *impression* of emotion or intellect will allow people to be within it decisively, not straining from it to some other attainment.

62. The historical persistence of margins makes them presently of one kind of use, to seduce the addicted eye.

63. The right hand margin is very strong in western civilization. It is established, rigidly, by rhyme and meter, not by some other form of justification, justification of form.

64. Yes, you would and could do all those things; you already have. If the person had no writing, you would have to begin with *that* standardization. You are not compelled to explain something which does not need explanation; again you are giving yourself something to need because you like having the lack of it.

66. A question mark six words long!

76. The resemblance is in the genes; that they have been passed on is evident in your mention of the predecessors. However, the mention is just another sentence.

78. No, it is not part of 'the process' until the process is named; then it is.

80. Writing would remain the metaphor that it always is, standing for its possibility.

81. Content is altered by all, which it is not separate from; especially, because often most obviously, its operation.

89. The more suddenly a term appears (appears to have appeared) the less we take it for a place-holder. In this way, words can appear to be within the function of great intrinsic desire.

90. Nouns reveal verbs. Nouns conceal verbs. — Verbs expend nouns.

91. Without the power to think or to speak, you could still push a button and get off at the sixth floor. This is what is meant as the word 'eye' secretes its verb; though it does not depend on that.

94. Having the thought that form exists, you have the fact that it does. This operation, seeming to prove itself, *supports* itself.

98. You would proceed by lining up all the nouns and changing their order until you were satisfied. Only your satisfaction would show for it.

104. Asking this question has changed you so severely that you don't bother to answer it.

112. That is a poem is a language is a stubborn idea because we persist in identifying with its function as a mode. The idea that 'vocabulary' has a plural is already a construct, and is already removed from *vocabulary* which it nevertheless appears to hover within.

114. Four uses of language only reduce the language to four impressions of it.

115. The formulation of your idea of the hill is a consequence of language, and the hill may be altered by your ideas of it. This only *seems* to make the hill exist; something it does effortlessly, while your thinking has reduced you. You continue to confuse your perceptions, your thoughts and the words which for you are their vehicle, with 'the hill' and 'the planet',

things which do not have to speak to exist.

117. Go to Paris.

118. Punctuation is usually part of a configuration; it shares its meaning. When a punctuation mark is "lost", nothing is really lost, there is no less than before; the meaning of the configuration *shifts*. Signs are not as separate as they appear to be when we examine them singly. Each sign contributes. A sign, before it contributes, is a possibility; it is that which makes us speak of it as pure, its state before it involves.

119. *The Chinese Notebook* is like prose in all respects.

123. Confusion ignites work.

130. A historian will not have much use for *Maximus* as long as he has its sources; he will speak, differently, as an equal. It was the availability of Pound's sources, the books and ideas and experiences, things which he *wanted* available, that led and permitted so many to disagree with him.

132. Anyone denying the possibility of referentiality is quitting the writing game. Sounds do not so much differ in type, as they provide a substance for recognizing meaning(s), which do.

141. *The Chinese Notebook* is not a poem; though it does question itself, though it is obsessive, though its mechanics produce and procure a partly vertical structure, though it is sometimes aware of itself as a poem and lets the reader know it, though it

143. Its personality is marked by what is left out because so much has been left in.

149. 'Poem', 'philosophy', 'metaphysics', 'criticism': nouns. These are among the states we leave when we write.

150. The definition of poetry is not distorted because you want it to include its contemplation. Each word (an integer with a hidden radical) already does that for itself; there is nothing to distort where distortion is wonderfully part of the function.

151. Literature is not limited to sequences or words.

153. A work makes a formal assertion as soon as it is.

155. You wrote "As always, the intention of the creator defines the state in which the work is most wholly itself" because you wanted to build up a great deal of certainty, some certainties which you hoped to link by their proximity, to *make* it be true.

156. Whatever you question, you have said.

159. Definitions would continue to be changing all over the place.

160. A medium does not "demand" anything, unless it be the furtherance of its mode.

162. "I" would not.

164. You would make that question less vague by transferring it somewhere else. The action of doing so would be its only answer.

170. A work's intentions are concealed by its imperfections. And the imperfections are its world.

171. It appears to us that a work, say, was intended as a good sonnet, but that it fails. The place where it was published may, as one factor, indicate the intention; the years since earliest sonnets were written will be a factor influencing our judgement. Considering intention, the work is a clue.

173. Intentions can be judged; but it is the nature of a work, and one of its appeals, that it will not interfere, will not help us with that judgement.

179. You can extend the term poetry. You could insist that the proposed event is a shoe. You would change the term only slightly by that one extension.

180. Poetry is not *a* condition. It is a class of possible uses for language. The word "poetic" is a little more precise, which helps us avoid its use, and at other times allows us to use it insultingly in speaking of a listless product. The noun is larger.

181. The attention to structure, to the work's gradual and careful performance. The worrying would be only a meaning, an aura.

182. Poetry is possible as a topic, a consequence, without the poem; the consequence would be a more murky theory. If we say "the poem" is the presence of an argument for something, then "poetry" points to the fact that we are arguing.

183. Language characterizes the man as long as we assume that he chooses his. It is the prevalence of the pronoun, which we notice, and which makes us wish to see each as a (kickable) noun.

184. Language characterizes man because we can only occasionally see past our mouths.

185. If we say so.

186. The same sentence in two contexts: (1) two sentences, (2) the same sentence. The context assigns meaning to the sentence; we recognize it. (1) The simple thing is repeated, assigned another job; (2) the simple thing is the same, but we notice that it does different work.

189. Robert Kelly writes poems, makes writing. From my reading, the former is far more important to him.

190. Ronald Silliman.

191. Knowing the vocabulary, either specifically or generally, we can see what has been used. In this way, each poem speaks of itself; we begin to make judgements about the poet, a personality capable of such work.

203. Strict structures for indeterminacy often falsify in pretending to be more ego-less, a personal concern which will not escape being one. But the artist may enjoy his hidden structure, which is not different from enjoying an overt one, except that overt structures have been drained of pleasure for the easily bored. Structures which announce their newness work insofar as they tire us quickly of our boredom; the justification for a work with a hidden form is that it has a relatively good chance of doing that.

205. They are the same: remember. They are different: remember.

211. It would be infinitely rare.

218. Like 'before' and 'after', the words 'buildup' and 'resolution' seem to fix points of an experience (reading) in time. Each point of the reading experience is only present, whether or not it is experienced as containing memory or expectation.

219. Words such as opposites are especially paired, seem to support each other. This is a statement about human nature.

This Predilection for the mind in art.
Where did I get it?

Structure is physical combination.

Economy maintains material, accepting it to structure.

Structure adumbrates materials. But necessity.

Structure is enthused with materials.
Structure is terminal; no surround.

A structure which does not reach of itself for support, is massive. After this, duration is a function of attention.

The words stubbornly insist on their place in the structure. Structure insists on their insistance.

Structure determines — machinates — senses. No thing gets sense without an endowment from structure.

The structure of words is their nascence.

Materials only burnish thought, structure.
Language underpins.

No aura surrounds structure. This constitutes its origin, its responsibility in perpetuation.

An intensification of any effort produces structure.

Thought is the mind's implement for locating structures. The mind retains some, assuming a personality.

Structure's *aim* in relation to content is to clean it of meaning.

In composition, certain ideas about altering the structure, undercut all need to do the work.

Structure is clean. It aligns the cacographic necessities, revives them.

All writing tends to its horizon: structure. (Not a limit; rather, the aura of the total gestures written and, over and through that, amplified.)

Attention to structure encourages the vertical subtleties.

Structure intercepts with no other textural element. They succumb in relation.

The one imperative is structure.

Structure (like any single word: noun more than adjective? verb more than adverb? noun more than pronoun? preposition more than article? Probably) points (at) itself.

Structure: no question of essences. Essence shines from materials, produced in light of the reading. Structure is, tension over balance.

Structure neither acts, nor is it an active, nor does it receive. It is a delicate stubborn effect produced under the permanence of the relations. It is not related; it stands.

How does it mean? Structure exerts power, which it cannot withdraw.

Structure has no poles, no extremes, no ends. Its balance is held between its side.

Structure is verified as a language, a code, is verified. We test it not by pursuing it but by pushing it; each structure must hold, against our critical effort, to the site it claims, otherwise it lies in its waste of space.

The structure of the materials are inseparable. They are the effort.

Structure is the one thing.
Structure is non-indictable. It is an urge manifest.

Structure is necessarily tautological.

When the structures emerge the materials arrive. When the materials converge, the structure has emerged.

If perception, the structure, doesn't come through language, there is no evidence that it has come through thought.

Structure leaves no time for an other thing because it withdraws to where it is, and is then found to be exactly where it must be allowed to remain.

Structure executes a project.

There is an element of life in structure which is absent from all other life.
Structure is the altogether latent of possibilities. Its presence. When it is reached.

And structure is nomenclature; a meeting. It is absent. Before and after. Structure hovers: its presence in the absence it empties.

Structure bends the line of sight, sometimes only very slightly, sometimes acutely. Thus it is recognized.

I, a private and concrete individual, hate structures, and if I reveal Form in my way, it is in order to defend myself.

LANGUAGE
MIND
WRITING

The fact that language as writing and language as speech are entirely separate is evident in the fact that they contribute to entirely separate sorts of work. They are separate because they do not occupy the mind at the same time. A thought in the mind may unite them, or a thought in the mind may aim to unite them, but they are not united in thought. Thought is the separation of language as writing from language as speech. Language is not, or never, difficult. It is the expression of life by life, the excelsior of a moment without the perpetuation of that moment, without the perpetual intrusion of that moment. If we follow the line of language into life we find that it encounters the body as speech, we find that it encounters the mind as writing. And it is, solipsistically, these encounters which give it its two definitions. When speech employs writing to make itself manifest, it is laughable, and when writing employs speech to make itself manifest, it is an excuse for a stronger gesture of the mind in the direction of life, thought in the directions of action. The work is in the thought, no matter which exit it chooses or, no matter to which exit it is forced, by the necessities, to default. There is never any absence of thought, but there is in writing its excellence, in speech its use, its use with perhaps an occasional perfecting. The distance between writing and speech is the distance between the surveyor of the land and the land. If language perpetuates itself in a world it is effortless, if speech or writing do so, it is in effort, by effort and, in the case of writing, for effort. There is no reason to externalize either of these facts, or quadrants, or gestures. Neither

is exterior to another. Externalization is the detriment of
language, of mind, of writing. There is something drastic in the
magnitude of our thought of these things, and it is such that
it does not permit them to separate except in thought, wherein
they are entirely separate. It is mind which teaches us where we
are wrong in writing. It is writing which teaches us wherein
the languages are wrong, wherein a language is wrong. And it
is language which, when an attentive tool, criticizes the obtrus-
ive forms of the mind, and sharpens it, or them, making it
that tool which separates all speech from thought, all speech
from writing, and writing the arbiter of their graceful resub-
missions. Our premise is the separation of the functions of
words in the world. Sometimes they exist in the mouth, some-
times they exist in the mind, and sometimes they exist on
the page. If they have appeared to exist between one and
another of these sites, it is because we have slurred our
thought. If they have appeared to be the same in one place
and in another, it is because our minds have been made too
weak to reckon changes. And if we have thought them the
same, we have not, by definition, thought. Thought is the
particular differences of its particulars. The equatability, in
part, of speech and writing, would appear to appear in part
because of their coexistence as two of the most particularly
noticeable among the particulars of thought. Where we have
three nouns in the language we have three things which we have
noticed to be separable, and where we have thought, soft
thought, we notice in its the reducibility of terms to the
softened absence of edges, the clinging mortality of identificat-
ion. We notice the excellence of a distinction when we recog-
nize the usefulness, within the world, of its separable terms.
We only need to know what we think, in order to act, but
we know that this article of intentions, which animates art,
would reduce so much of the world to stopping. The identity
of the uses of language is apparent only to those who do not
actually use it, those who, for example, speak without thinking,
those who write without thinking, think without writing,
or one person of some sort such as these. There may be a
reason to produce the language as a gesture and if there is

then that reason is writing, but there can be no reason to reduce the languages to a language, nor could there be a reason to produce one language in the direction of the forms of another, unless that reason is laziness, or default. Language is as strong as mind is as strong as writing is as strong as language. As long as one of these separable functions remains separate it is as strong as the interior strengths common to the others and itself, but the imitation of one function of language by another begins to manifest the unfortunately functioning confusion of one form of confusion as another.

We project as language the interest of our minds in thought. The language is the peculiar function of the mind in which it immerses itself when it thinks, and in order to think. A language is any gesture which the mind repeats in order to understand itself. Later, in order to disseminate that understanding, in order to see it, the mind reduces a language to a speech, or to a writing. But the language is the mind in contact with itself and most particularly with its understanding of, that is, with its dealings with, itself, and its understanding with, and its dealings of, itself. Language marks the presence of our strange default in relation to life, that we think about it. It presents us to ourselves in view of our thought, as if we were life's gimmick. This failure is our failure to penetrate language in thought, in life. This failure poses us abjectly at the edge of our imminent and delayed failure, our imminent but delayed future. We fail the language when we don't permit it as its own mode of thought, as a mode of thought, when we as it were exact from it a penance for that its existence which we nevertheless encourage, and when we make it do the work for another mode of thought, or for no thought at all, for the very distinct presence of the absence of thought. A language is a tool of thought, the mind is the languages at work, and the difference between mind and thought is the difference between name and function. Language is a use we make of our time when we choose to live in it. In these ways, or for these reasons, we begin to treat the language as an encumbrance, an abuse, and we then so readily get to be the ones who abuse it. The language is one of the verbs for us that as we use it can justify its taking from us the unreliable place of the verb to be. We imagine what it would or could be like to be more spectral or more calm in the space of what can there be at best the vicinity of being, and there, then, is the region of the habitable uses of language, in the space of the lifetime. We rush to find ourselves in the habitable regions of the language, and others rush to find themselves even near such places, for there the language touches the language, the uses for the language touch the uses of it, and the person is a whole entity at the end of the apt expression of the whole of a thought. The languages make possible for us the reasonings, the forms of reasoning, in the mind, and they make possible the unreasonable problems of frail, broken, incomplete, or otherwise damaged, thoughts, the lesions in thought. The language is, though, properly the excellent tool of excellence in the mind, in acts in the and of the mind, in the mind's thoughts, in the mind's actions in the other languages, the outer languages of the other world. The languages are within the mind a community of the uses of the mind, its efforts within itself and going beyond itself, perhaps leaving the mind but never the language behind. The language is that vehicle of which it is meant that it make for the mind a place in the world. To the extent that the world is a receptacle for language, it is the occasion for, the occasion of, the mind. To that extent to which the world receives the languages, to that extent exactly, the world is a book. Mind begins in language to constitute for itself an expression of itself, and in this way language began, and in this resides the completion of a thought, its excellence in complete articulation, its excellence an excellence in articulate completion, because the beginning of the language is also the completion, the beginning of the mind. It is difficult to think about the language objectively, with what in the language is called objectivity, because the language is the mode of thought among other things also of the language, the thought of language, also, and, also, the language of thought. We would have to say, attributing to ourselves the simplicity of the statement, that language is not separate from the mind, nor is the mind the sum of the languages, nor is it controlled by them. The language intercepts the mind. That is the notion of the language in the mind. The language does the work of thought as it enters itself or as it enters the world. Writing exemplifies language as it performs those works of thought which enter thought, and speeches are the form of the languages when they blatantly and, frankly, too frequently, enter the world. Nothing is fatal in the vicinity of language, mind, and writing. And it is also too commonly felt that either might be fatal, to itself, to the self, to the social self, or to thought. The language is not precious, or sacred, or a vessel. It exemplifies a mind in the world. The language is the pact that the mind keeps with itself, and when the mind keeps a pact with the world, it engages a language with which to do it. If the beauty of the mind is something which engages thought, then the language, a language, is the, is an, example of that. It appears to us that the language is the end of everything and the beginning of anything. If there is a reason for forgetting it is the language and not the future, and certainly not the completely imaginary past, and the language is the instrument of forgetting, its implement. There is no need to understand the beginning or the beginnings of language, because the beginning, the beginnings, of language, constitute the origin of the completion of the mind as an object, its initiation as a tool, and the language was something which was there as either of these other things happened, or were happening, to complete themselves. Perhaps some things are more perfect than the language and perhaps something is more perfect than the mind, but gradually we begin to doubt ourselves, each doubts each, and the assertion closes on itself, the pariah of speech. It is not the style of language to exclude itself from thought, and that is the definition of style. The language is a special and perfectible thing, special because we know it, because we know in it, and perfectible because we come close to it, and, over it, and, pass it with the language as that excellent weapon of lazy self, in the teeth. The language is not sentimental, or it is the excelsior of sentiment, when it lives. The language is the present without qualifiers. The language does not qualify anything until it is forced to by some idiocy within the world. Released to be itself, that is, being what it would be without that release the need for which we demand for it by our lazy and insistent ways, being there separate from stupidity, and articulate about it, the language makes the nouns live with the verbs, that is all it does, and it does that very well. When we wish to know something about the language we use it, and our use of it tells us more than we had thought we would be asking, because our asking is full of the faults, and language is full with the excellences of its use, that excellence which permits it to be of use. We too often manage to make the language work because we are inattentive to anything else, to everything, else. But the language is a special tool, and, one which does not specialize, and its perfection is always its solidity within, whichever is most immediate of its own gestures, and its gestures make us used to it.

We would not say that the mind is the same as or that it is different from the language, or a language, or the many languages. Languages are the evident portions of minds. The mind is the favored location of the languages when the languages are preferred to be doing their favored, their best, work. The mind is the site of the language when it is most perfectibly the language, the place where a language most and most explicitly perfects itself, and you don't work in the mind without breaking the mind into thoughts, and thought is the explicit early action of a language, but the mind will not relent. The most resilient of factors is the fact of the mind. The mind is the legacy of the acts of the languages, but it is also and, incidentally, more interestingly, the locus of the languages in labor. The mind is the instructing within a life. With memory it is the instructions, and with life it is the simple, temporary, solid, and solitary, construction of the instructions in the life. The language is the presences of the vocabularies and the grammars and the mind is the sentences in the sense of the carrying out of the instructions implicit in the presence of the active vocabulary, the acting grammar, and the instrumentation of each by, and in relation to, each. The mind is the actions in thought of a life, and if memory is its periphery then in those places the mind is a center, an

activity which, at its best, diminishes into itself, a soft sharp
point of moving focus, without exaggeration, without
extension, and if interior to anything, interior to it only in
default. The language does not ever use the language as a
vehicle for trading out of itself. The language is occasionally
or perhaps frequently made to do that work, that sort of
work, but by persons living entirely then exterior to the
mind, their own mind. The mind is the focus of a life in the
world. The language is the light of the mind, the point of its
pointed focus in the world. Mind is that device of perpetual
motion the existence of which death exists to reinforce if not
to prove. The mind in the pursuit of mind, or, mind in pursuit
of the mind, these are among the strongest urges which fasten
upon a life, or upon which any life fastens. The mind is the
evidence of forms, it is their making evident and, making them
evident, in order to make them evident, it forms the languages
in the worlds of the lives of the humans. It is simple to rest in
consideration of other things but all considerations rest, in the
end, within the mind as their origin, and in the mind as their
conclusion. The mind tolerates no illusion and so the language
has about it no illusions, such that where the language
exemplifies illusion it evaporates the mind. When we think
about the mind, the mind talks, and when we write about the
mind it is the mind that writes, and if we talk about the mind
it is, then, the mind which talks. It is in these ways, and in those
other ways of which it may be said that this way of the mind
represents them, in which we come to recognize that the
worlds reside in the mind, and that the mind does not only
represent them. When the mind is charged with the task of
representing a world, then the world is in default of its own
presence to the mind. The mind is the function of the mind,
etcetera, and the etcetera is the usual failure of the world to
account for the presence of the equatabilities within the mind.
The world is usually not up to that. This is because the mind
is the pure function of function, as we experience it, because
its function is purified in the actions of its functioning, and
because its exemplification is its loss in the streets of the usual
minds of the world. There is no excuse that the mind ever

makes in the world, and that is because the mind does not
ever touch the world, and that is because of the space between
the spaces that habitually touch the world. The world derives
its strength from the mind, and that is the simple fact of the
human presence in the world, and without it, the mind would
derive its strength solely from the mind because of the absence
of the human in the worlds. There is no reason to equate
anything else, but the mind's constant equatability with the
mind belies the presence of anything else within the world.
The world equals the world, etc., but the actions of equata-
bility occur and then exist within the mind. The mind is the
locus of all the human action of the world. It moves the
material of the world, and is itself only material if it is dead.
The mind is the world's volution, or the world is its circum-
ference. The mind is a still point amidst the horizons of the
world, because thought is vertical, and the verticalization of
language in writing its nascent nadir, as object. The mind is the
workplace of the living. Only the dead work only in the world.
The differences between the languages has only small recourse
to a mind, which uses them as extents of its resources, and
makes of any one of them, in its use of that one, one equatable
with the others, lost there, and, of no more importance than
that, its use, and the occasion of its use. The mind is the
occasion of its use. Otherwise there is no mind. There are no
mistakes made by the mind because everything that the mind
does is its work and in that it is not mistaken. There are, how-
ever, frequent mistakes made in the mind by the life which
surrounds it, by a life which surrounds it, by the or a world, by
thought without thought as its object, or by a language in the
hands of something other than of a mind. The details of the
mind, inside of the mind, are perfect, its actions are perfect,
and these are the sorts of things meant by perfection. The
intrusions of the worlds are the origin of any faulting in, in
any faulting of, the mind. But a mind which has first strength-
ened itself with its own devices and its own acts, and, where
necessary, been absorbed quite totally in and by them, might
become and be a mind capable of thought, capable of habit-
ation by languages, or capable of writing, without repeating

and thereby inspiring the furtherance of the faults of the worlds without minds. It is the fault of the world that the mind fails, and the strength of the mind that it comes to know that. It is by a kind of isolation from the world which is yet entirely attentive to it, that the mind does perfectly the work of the mind, discerning in itself the longest reaches of its actions, and outside of itself the short appurtenances which can encumber it with hesitations. Outside of the mind exist for example those mistakes of the language, which we have mentioned, and which are in fact the mistakes in contacts between the mind and the world. It is necessary for the mind to remember its place in the mind before the life takes the mind to its place in the world. The mind is the world before the internal mistakes of the world, and with them the mind is the locus of the functioning of the languages of the world. Each person lives in a space bounded by thought. Each thought is bounded by language, or, more accurately in the realms of action, it is the languages that mediate between the points of the person and the layer of thought. And writing is itself not beyond language, within this present thought in metaphor. Writing is the point of mind reaching through thoughts to languages, or, writing is the point of mind living itself, as explicitly and distantly as possible, through the languages to the goal of some anticipated and then manufactured thought. The mind is the use of every thing, without metaphors or distances, although it is through the sharpened, acute, perpendicular distancing of its uses from itself, that it achieves those clear notions of things as they are, and which make it of use to thoughts, to languages, and to the perpendicular distributions of writings upon the flat and blatant horizons of the world.

We begin, first of all, when we write, to extort from life, from the life of the mind, and from the minds of the lives in the world, the explanation or the explanations for the existences and the meanings of the existences of the written things in the world. And suddenly and much later we question their perfectibility, and in that perfectibility that immaculate thing which we notice, the perfectibility or the thoughts of the perfectibility, of the world. When the mind

focuses itself through the exaggerated and dense focal point
of arranged language, or languages, it is then that it writes.
The pressurization of the language by the mind produces writ-
ing, and the pressurization of a language by a mind is the result
of the mind's effort to produce through a language its own
maximum elongation of itself in relation to what is to it one
among the possible objects. It is perhaps contradictory that,
or it is perhaps only that two contradictorily metaphorical
expressions of this situation exist in that, the most absolute
of attainable directnesses is produced through that which it
is most direct in passing, a pressurization of that. Writing may
perhaps most evidently be the mind's perfection of the lan-
guages but it is also, through the languages, the perfection, by
life in the world, of a mind, of the mind, of the minds. The
mind is the thing which does work and it is at the same time the
work that that thing does. It is a form, a structure, or, more
exactly, more certainly more than one of each and all of
them, and it is also a group of tools, the actual, past and po-
tential organizations of those tools, their uses within itself and
in the world, and their final extension in the facts of writing.
We sometimes falteringly assume, then, that writing, in lan-
guage, contains images of the mind. But this is as false, if only
a little more difficult, than the easily held impression that it
is the task of writing to hold images of the world, as if the
world for some reason required within itself images of itself.
Writing does inevitably, and may exactly, bear impressions of
that world or those worlds from within which it becomes. It
does this with a kind of genetic inevitability born from and
alive within the processes of giving birth. Writing is the product
much more of work than of gestation, even the thought which
is a part of its production being much more a diligence at work
than an attentiveness in waiting, but still, and certainly, it
produces as it becomes an object something which resembles
the mind which made it, the life, the lives, and the world of
which the mind is most emphatically a part. This is one of
the primary truths of a writing, one of the primary tests of
its truth, that it carry within itself and, that is, within the ways
it works, the impressions accurately retained, of the world and

the particulars of the world, within which it was made. The judgement of the results of such a test, of the accuracy of writing in relation to its world, is subtle, as finely tuned as the writing itself, and as subtle as the mind which reads in judging and which judges when it reads. And these relationships obtain because it is a mind which writes, and because writing is a mind's most direct and most continually direct access, along the lines of language and by the use of thought, to its object in the mind, and to its possible erection within that mind of that mind as though it were a place or a thing in a place in the world. So that writing is truly the focus of the mind in the world and also, the focus of the world, through a mind, and then in that, or in another, world. And writing is if at all only secondarily the point, the durable and enduring point, of that focus. Primarily it is the work of the mind, pitched against its excellence, against its own most excellent facets, and in the world, of the mind, of thoughts in language, and of the world. Primarily writing is the focusing of the mind. It is the uses for and of itself which a mind locates in focusing, whatever the object of that focus, and whether it have one or not. Writing is therefore the mind's processing upon itself of the maximum of its critical functions, in order to produce writing, in order to produce meaning, and in order to produce the mind. Writing produces the mind. It is as though the question of writing entered always the equation of thought or of mind the way an equals sign enters the world. Here, of course, the equals sign is only an example of any sign, but metaphorically so, because it is a sign which divides as it writes, as a sign with two sides that are in reality one side, as a sign of the whole as, with, and by its parts, a sign in which, momentarily, the dimensions display themselves as one, in the thought in the mind. Writing is the tribute that a life makes, to the world, of the perfectibility of a life in the world. Writing is the tribute that a life makes, in the world, of the perfectibility of any life, in any world. There aren't any artifacts in the world that the mind hasn't made, and writing is the best of them, and writing is the least of them, because writings are the excellent functionings of something which does so in order

to function. In these ways the pieces of writing that do these
things are alive. If writing were something which simply hap-
pened to the mind the mind would be simply more content,
or if the mind were simply something which happens to the
writings, then writings would be only improved or, perhaps,
merely improvable, but, because writing and the mind are, at
their best, individually and collectively, not separate, the
world and the worlds may be said to be better, simply, with
the mind, or the minds, the writing, or the writings, strongly
within them. It is writing which brings the mind to the mind.
The mind may of course do this for itself directly, but that
we call enlightenment, itself the pursuit of the mind, by the
mind, and with tools. Writing is never an end. When it is
treated as such, or looked to as such, and very often it is,
then it falls short of the mind, the thoughts in the life of the
languages, and the minds in the lives. When writing is an end
to writing, it is an end to the mind. When writings are an end
to writing, then that is that. When writing ends in writings,
tautologically enough, writing ends. Writing can't be an object
because the world is a world of verbs and to write is a thing
that someone does. Writing is an action in the world. Writing
is the mind, any mind with language in its mind, and active
in the world. The pursuit of excellent writing is the pursuit
of excellent actions. Writing is the work of the mind without
display, without exegesis, and without contact, other than
with itself. Writing is the end of the world when it seeks itself
because the world seeks itself through mind, and the mind
seeks itself, frankly, in writing. Writing is something that
doesn't stop. Writing, as old as a definition of the mind, is
that part of the mind which does not stop. Only of the mind
itself, and of writing, can it be said that its pursuit of the
mind is permanently exemplary. Either is, obviously, the
permanent exemplification of itself, and each is also, and
tacitly, in some ways the exemplification of the other.
The particularizations of these modes of similarity, these
similarities between one mode and another, belie their singu-
larity. Writing is the particular destiny of the mind in the
world. Writing is the particular destiny, and also and at the

same time the particular density, of language in the world. Writing is its own acts, and in that way, or, perhaps more accurately, in those ways, it avoids nothing of everything in the world. Writing enters the world at its center, because that is where writing exists, and it is therefore that writing never leaves that location, where it can and does work, and where its example is at least equally evident to all portions, and to all points on the perimeters, of the worlds. Writing can avoid the pathologies of the world, by remaining at its center, or it can make the much more common mistakes of reconnoitering the world. The reasons for the mind's use of writing as an instrument of foray into the world, are legion, but they can be perhaps also accurately reduced to the preponderance of preponderant egos without minds. Writing is the answer to the questions of the uses of the mind at work.

It is difficult to conclude that of which each statement has been a conclusion. Perhaps it will prove most naturally pointless of all to be trying to be doing that. It is difficult to conclude that of which each assertion, and any and each portion of each assertion, has been a conclusion. These conclusions have been not of the form of those most and more usual conclusions, which are dead, but rather they are of a form of conclusion in that each thing which has been said has been a tool at work. A tool at work makes its point, it concludes in that work, for that moment or those moments, its existence in the world. That is its existence, that it does its work, and that it is witnessed, that is its conclusion. Perhaps it would conclude itself without witness if we were without minds, but because we have them and when we use them, the conclusion of language, of mind, and of writing, is in the mind. We do not, however, by saying that, forget that each finds its most excellent existence, within the limits, if we were to call them that, of its own use, its own possible uses. It is a simple enough thing that if we permit to each thing its own existence, and if we do that also in the mind, we may clear a way to clarity, and live our lives with the diligence of being in the center of the cleansed portions of each of our acts.

CENTURY ARTICLE 80

1

reading	language	writing
language	writing	reading
writing	reading	language

language	reading	writing
reading	writing	language
writing	language	reading

2

reading	language	writing
reading	writing	language

language	writing	reading
language	reading	writing

writing	reading	language
writing	language	reading

-or-

performing	language	writing
writing	language	performing

writing	performing	language
performing	writing	language

language	writing	performing

language   performing   writing

3

writing   language   reading b
writing   reading   language   c

reading   writing   language   c
language   writing   reading a

language   reading   writing a
reading   language   writing   b

Mallarmé

Dice = paper submission

The swelling values of attention emit few words, total world

page control — words' secular grace — surfeit

The pen vibrates for moves; or attach; the crescent divulgence conclusion or each motion, emote

Words turn in through a page diggingly, make troughs of secure settlement for stasis movement

sturm und drag — the language obediently perfect, gotten up — morphological emission

A wave of nerve passes into the white back of all black

stopping stoppers squared remission
        dimension, pace, flattery

sore laces albeit the moment in space

The end cornered in each corseted beginning, the flack excessively upright, the tonal evanescence, the tradition at once (traction), the fervence

Imagined diagrams

Cooleridge

Daughter / Wife /
    Mistress

"A throw of intention". . .

The desire, that the water would write against the boat

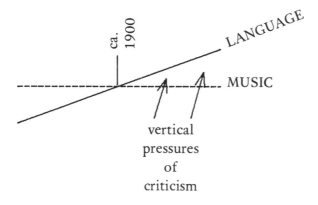

vertical
pressures
of
criticism

Attire premonitions developed at the time of M's attention. These were/he summarily conditioned in the Tombeau de. The world developed only very very slowly outside of among the peripheral gestures of this region. Recourse to the black tie was donned summarily. The irises, glacial or of eyes, took this minute task. The substitute for attention was bound in attire. No sequence wavered, trotted. The active servitude piled into taxis, moved the stubborn era, evaded more prescient motive. The streets were dark and two-armed beneath this tribulation. The toast was taken daily, au matin. Cabs immediately, after thought, opened to purveyors of tilting dialogue. Then it was early for reading of signs and late for dismissal. Dismal times fluctuated among the pads. Two-sided evocation took his time, the time taken to oneside fleet tracts. M woke up, his presence sudden in among white. The time was times multiplied. The facets replete.

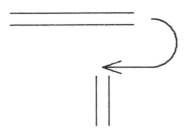

Distribution and configuration
of, and.

In the book the few choices are taken by the letter a. The letter regulates the perfunctory deployment of the page. Each space, if called, is initially darkened by the letter a. This contributes to the cloud which moreover makes of the page a performable space. The page empties of light. The material page is obedient to structure, its dark dominatrix. This transmits the feeling that feeling is feeling. Otherwise the old vowels survive intact. The moment when the page describes this is of no importance. The inscription is lost, perhaps lines, before that. The requirement is study. No requisite is required. When the letter punctuates the page, reply is implicit. The glance is dark, of all. The two minds, page and, earlier, letter, vary the pleasure. Each footed intrusion of letter over page, each extrusion of letter by page, the maculate synthetic.

The concept of subject is used here in the same sense as in modern philosophy (for example, in Ernst Cassirer's Philosophy of Symbolic Forms, particularly in its third volume), that is to say, as a member of the antinomy object-subject. In this sense, the subject perceives the object, acts upon the object, makes the object, and so on. The subject in this sense is that to which all mental representations or all operations and actions are attributed. Unfortunately, in the English language there is a danger of confusion. Although common usage knows such derivatives as "subjective" and "subjectivity," the term "subject" is mostly used, when there is a question of art,

semiotics, and so forth, in the sense of "subject matter." This danger of confusion cannot be avoided. The concept is too important to be replaced by circumlocutions or by terms that are only partly synonymous. For instance, it would be tempting to avoid the language difficulty by replacing the antinomy object-subject by the antinomy "it"-"I." But that would be misleading because it would conceal the antinomy which is inherent in the concept of subject itself: the subject can be not only "I" but also "thou" — it can be not only the first-person subject but also the second-person subject. Because of its psychological connotations and of its intrinsic paradox-icalness, the antinomy "ego"-"other ego" cannot help either.
Jiři Veltruský, *Dramatic Text as a Component of Theatre*

Poetic reference is primarily determined, then, not by its relationship to the reality indicated, but by the way it is set into the verbal context.
Jan Mukařovský, *Poetic Reference*

                                                                    Deictic
Directly provoking by argument. Showing or pointing out directly; direct; proving directly.
(able to show directly; to show) (serving to show or point out; to show)

        *

Refuting by proving the opposite. Serving to refute; applied to indirect modes of proof.
(to refute)

                                                                   Elenctic

All of this to thrust ourselves into the heart of obsolete things. To decipher the contours of the banal as puzzle, to discover the figure of a hidden 'William Tell' among wooded entrails, or to answer the question 'Where is the bride?'
Walter Benjamin, *Dream Kitsch*, 1927

Thus, for example, in all probability the color of the handle of the hammer will remain unnoticed. But a moment of decisive reversal can occur when we start to look at a practically designed object in a different way, when we observe the object itself and for itself. At that moment a peculiar change will take place—at least in our eyes. Above all those properties of the object which have no relation to the particular aim and were previously overlooked, which in some cases were not even perceived at all (for example, its color), will come to our attention. But even those properties that have a practical use and were formerly the center of attention now appear to us in a different light. Being deprived of the relation to the aim lying *outside* the object, these properties enter into relations with one another within the object itself, and the object appears to us as if it were constructed from its own properties bound into a unique and integral whole.

Jan Mukařovský, *The Essence of the Visual Arts*, 1944

Speaking of the autonymous voice only M had it first. The rubrics of paged Grecs fragments frags. On the lonelier aspect of the fan over the lintel, this dispersal. The anechoic words. The anechoic words. The anechoic, words at last in space with no meat for silence. The distant wherewithal *plunders* the present, a. Discourse is limited to a speaker. The audience is unwitting, glad or caught away from the perseverent act. M over came our selves, M in order to write words. Neither bridges nor lapses, the turnpike at multiple locii. Only the encore laced out of probability. M the man. The farce a word for that word, for example. M fleeting away. Mr M. The colorish traces of the text or Mr M. The furtherance of explicit gender implicit in fowl, in lilies, in death, in dearth of dearth. The pressure of M in the immediate venn diagram. The loss of M from M, to the betterment. A release from tonal requirements not lost! battened onto the present emassment of dark on the light, the preference for might, of might. M over and above. M most nascent. M. M the inveterate man. Or the color (sic) of ink on and over stone. The settlement of verbs, the noun.

(The pronoun.)

A definition of the space in which thought procures thought:
this space has a specific title. It is occupied by integers and by
motion. It doesn't talk yet. This space uses itself *as* time, a
byproduct of motion. This *space* runs down. It stops itself
from being *over*heard. In this space the material of thought
rests (period.) on the angular chords of motion (see above).
This space is wider than it is long, having been long for
too long. This space *is* limit. *This* space. This space, its num-
erous instances, its variously impacted motives, is not large.
cf.—Each thought materially reduces it. In a moment, chased
by perspective, it becomes small enough to weigh everything,
to be a *weight* of everything. This space, when subtracted
from all "other" space, does not reduce it. This space *moves*,
from one distance to another distance, without time *or* motion.
This space takes from the present only that percentage, of,
which the present has already done without. This space, it,
this space. This space takes its energy from the remainder.
This space bears no relation to any other, being in no respect
different. This space has only one dimension, the omni-dimens-
ion. It has begun to talk.

The speculation is always in relation to the audience, as, mas-
tery is to speculation. Or it is the question of, anyway, put
passively and upright. The aura sense interrupts this positively.
For this reason, the interruption is a speculative and timely
element. The absent element is more commonly the first
mentioned. This collusion. The purveyance of fact, as if, as,
sentiment. The voice broke over the triumphant broadcast,
leasing no elision. Signification flew into the nostrils, it was
language lacking. *The* erasure of *the* significant gesture. And
the absence that speculates. French for triumphant. The sur-
rounded erupt *in* = *what* they were reading. An infuriated
author. This pressure rereleases the vertical layers, lathed,
battered and finally, what shall one man say, erect! But the
temperature has remained constant. These methods of endear-

ment or response interchangeably enact the old writerly ideas. A vectorist submits his ideas to the council. The entire separate structuration, the most fallen. And when a *kind* of severance stages, the watery biceps relax and a mind stiffens for that pursued trenchant act. The motion of a word, a fact. There is a town in the west where this kind of thought is pursuant to the sun. Otherwise the enactable speculant falters, rusts the pump stops. And the leather attention to thought is thorough, from this premise no thing or time is taken. A weather goes back, return, speculation itself. Of course caresses the first premise, engages in that mistake. This accelerates a meaning for structure, is to say duration. Terminus in the rain. The quadrant on which life plots, the alterable approach of language to reproach, or the angle of a limb that is dead. This recent imagery substitutes for the better version of felt prescience, this verse, the oblate. *And the presence i-midst speculative vengeance.* The tract. Searching this version of irregularity, its midst, the template. Each fact buries the, *the*, world.

In the year 1900. 1900. The air was ok. The weather was perpetually inclement, a result of M's temperament. Others of people alive then (sic) found it possible to populate, survive. A kind of mellifluous sustenance prevailed. It is unique that a year became a century. Loss of interest in pursuit of all lost fans, an aggressive insistence on the structural emblematic a pyre. A future became probable in the mouths of three men, not yet named, not oracular or specific but mnemonically resurgent. For this space of time, albeit beyond it, the temperament became subject to the verb write, and transparent. Please take out of this the sense. The century was a week old, to the week, when direction became the imperative. After writing the worlds into the landscape, which happened with a death in Texas, some duration of lens, these things these things these things. The triumphs occurred in afternoons, swans at bay. Given a great shortage in paper, the bathrooms will remain of note. An amazing number of scientific hands flooded the available faces. Sky dropped all over, water succeeding where earth hath failed. A legislative note, *this* on over *this*, made possible the too future ecriture, the punctuation grace. It wasn't affordable but there was an idea involved. More of both please. Ore the irregular placement of the language in the social fray, the again of structure hopefully over way over fact. The first piece of furniture in the era of the entirely possible, the narcissistically potential, was the malicious or impossible *irregularity*. 21 years of in. It has never before happened that it end like this.

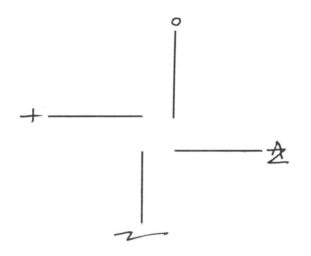

Four cardinal points of literary
effort (ordinal points of shadow).

IF WORDS HAD MEANING

I find that I have nothing to say, and I find that I feel no apology in saying that.

Most people don't write persistently, and almost none of those who don't wish they did.

There is between the at first willingly accepted and then later somewhat willfully encouraged estrangement from the effort, and an increasing disdain for the result, of writing, every reason for my not having written for what has been after all the relatively short period of a little over a year.

I had thought that I would perhaps say nothing, or next to nothing. I had thought that I would perhaps write nothing to say, as in some time I have written next to nothing; two poems, discarded, one article, the written draft completed, another article begun, and now this.

But there is something in me that writes. What is it?

It is me.

Or perhaps there is in me instead something which will avoid speaking, like this, formally, without having written.

There is in each of us in this belligerently literate society something which writes.

Writing is espionage in the mind.

It is cultivation, indiscreet cultivation.

There is nothing, now, here or elsewhere, that I have written, that makes me want to go on. It lost me so easily, almost as if there were better things to do.

"Why won't you listen to me? Why won't you let me develop the premise of honest utterance with feeling, as the basis of our relationship?"

That sort of thing.

I remember with what energy I used to write, with what considerable conviction. I was filled with the feeling of the wonderful sentence just completed; its balance, its accuracy, its considerable control, and its beauty. Oh wow. I got up, paced to the window, rushed back, got down a couple of more sentences, drank some bourbon, wrote some more, with such intensity, got up, bounced a ball off the wall two or three times, using up the energy, you know, standing there, thinking.

Thinking I was thinking.

It's all quantity versus resistance.

Why anyone would want to push a considerable quantity against any resistance at all is beyond me.

Quality is another matter.

It occurs best when other matters have quietened down. Quieten other matters. The quality is there. Mostly you just don't ever see the quality for the quantity. It's no easier to mobilize stupidity than insight, but it's commoner. No, actually, it's a hell of a lot easier. You know what I mean.

So many people nowadays are living for the present that there isn't enough to go around.

What's worse, there isn't enough room left on the left anymore. Dilettantes and real artists have been crowding over in that direction for years, so that this is a particularly acute problem for artists of all types.

The reason they've been moving over there is because it's easier to think and not, unfortunately, because it's possible to think better. It isn't. But it is much easier there to think better of oneself.

If you've been having any kind of trouble living, any kind at all, you should stop writing. It's the best thing for it.

This says something, perhaps something interesting, about the relationship between living and writing.

What is that relationship? And what, you may ask, is so interesting about it?

Writing is something that people who are alive are able to do. It's unfortunate, but many, many people go ahead and start writing long before they're really alive enough to have been ready to begin. As a result, they may not have the where-withal to write exceptionally well, or they may not yet have anything to say when they write. In either case the writing will have nothing alive in its matter or its means. And in certain very common cases, it will have nothing alive, and not even anything of life, in it anywhere at all.

This is very unfortunate for the writer and the writers, for the reader and the readers.

I feel as though here I were writing down to myself.

It's one of the most pleasant sensations I've experienced for quite awhile. There is something sensual about it, which I naturally very much like.

I'm writing for you what I think about things, and being out of the habit of writing, I find that I enjoy this simplicity of expression.

Beats hell out of the glottal irascible brogue of self-expression, which I had merely perfected to an art.

It warms my heart.

Most of our writing is impertinent. Demanding, and somewhat stupid, like brushing our feet and then putting our shoes on, and feeling good about it.

We have all written in order to see what we have written, to wear it with pride. But pride is no substitute for life, and no justification for anything.

Life requires, to begin, an integration of thought and feeling which few of us and seldom demand of our experience. We have all been content with less, in order to propose, for ourselves alone, perhaps, the choice expression, the beautiful phrase.

We have been happy with ourselves for the beauty of our solutions, not for long if at all questioning the very small size of the preferred problem.

I stopped to think.

We wanted to make something beautiful, and something new.

We did. I did. You did. He, she, it did. We did. You all did. They did.

There's nothing like fire to fuel the brain, and the brain is fire. Feelings rise from the fire like smoke. No one sees it, because no one obtains them.

I'd like to thank the people who have expressed a concern that I have stopped writing. Now I know who my friends are, and I know what one of their problems is.

We have our pride.

There's no mistaking any of us.

I had become so used to expressing, with accuracy and conviction, those feelings which I knew I had and yet had not felt, that I decided without thinking, or without awareness of my thought, to stop that expression.

One of us said that. Any one of us could have.

Unfelt literature is dead, and writing without feeling kills the writer. Writing without direct, unintellectualized feeling requires a problematic change in the state of all of the materials of that action, including the state of the one acting. Don't waste your time.

What is after all the simplest way to put a relationship between literature and life?

Isn't literature rather too often something with which we wash our hands of life after whatever we have been able to manage of living? Is that why we want it to be relatively, and perhaps even increasingly, antiseptic?

We lie to ourselves because we haven't thought about and haven't felt, what we're saying.

Putting it in print for others is a bit much. We could at least take some time first to put it in perspective for ourselves, and some time before that to put ourselves in perspective.

Literature suffers not half so much from literariness, which is after all only a surfeit of good grace, as it does from the religion of writing. There is a religiosity dyed into the fabric of our making art that makes of faith a blasphemy and of hope a charnel. It lays life waste.

The literary world is a small cloister of abbots so over-frocked with notions of their actions that they can pretend to themselves that they are naked, or transparent, or that they are making beautiful, before the cult of their own consumption.

Almost no one just writes. And to do so is perhaps impossible.

Most are so frightened that they have nothing to say, or that they have something to say, that they spend what little time they have just saying well.

I almost wish I had said this more poorly. I guess you haven't quite yet convinced me of the need for that.

We have all found ourselves angry with writers who have written about something, but badly. Perhaps it has been that anger which has pushed us to write well, whether about anything or not.

I find that I do have something to say. It comes from my thoughts and my feelings, and from my concern about their separation. I will say it only as well as is needed, and it is you, to whom I am speaking or writing, who determine the exact nature of that need.

You will determine if it is to continue, and I will help you, by doing this.

Finding that we have a jargon for every occasion, we have invented some new jargons, but without occasion. These new jargons have neither demanded nor required occasions.

We have argued that they are their own occasion. In this way we have tried to elevate the hollow, and have found that the hollow rises easily. Seeing it thus elevated we have said to ourselves that we have done an elevated thing or, even, that it was an elevated thing to have done, that it was elevated to begin with.

In short we have congratulated ourselves upon the ease with which we have lifted a weightless thing, while congratulating ourselves also upon its elevated status.

Occasionally, for diversion, or in the process, we have lifted our own weight, and let it fall.

There is no pretext for writing, but writing is full of pre-texts.

The only pretext for writing is the criticism of it.

Stand by your mind.

Your guts might stand by you, if they can stand you. And your feelings might just stand up to you, if you let them.

We all of us make the world small enough to manage. That's what we use the language for. That's what we've done with it.

Until you have something better to offer yourself you might just go on thinking that's enough. And until I have something much more to give to the world than that, I don't think I'll know anything of all that the language is really good for.

What I have written so far makes me feel that it will have been of more interest to those familiar with what I have written in the past than it will have been to those not so familiar.

It's as simple as knowing who your friends are.

I know what I'm doing here, and I'm doing it as at that spot in the bottom of a bowl, where liquid settles first. Once you know what you are doing you have at least a chance of doing it well. No one knows what they will do next but at least, knowing that, one has a better chance of doing it with ease and fullness.

Until you know and feel that you write better for those who have never read you than for those who have, you will to some degree be writing best only for yourself alone. There is no harm in that, but neither is there hopeful benefit.

What I am trying in part to write and speak about is idolatry of the word, an even worse program than the state legislation of literature. This idolatry comes inexcusably and without excuse, from within the lives of the persons who profess to make the writing. For the most part they don't know what they're doing. When they do, there is a slyness immediately discernable, and when they don't, there is a combination of meekness and pride that is revolting.

In its most negative sense, the word is the legacy of idolatry.

Writers have been its advocates. They continue to be its priests.

Writers, like other priests, have chosen this role because of the vestments, the sacristry, the shared religion, because of the sanctity of the role, its sometimes secular aura, and especially because of the liturgy.

They have fancied that they are making something new, in order to partake of the cult of the new. They have imagined that they are criticizing and subverting the prevailing systems, in order to touch through the only means whereby they have access to it, the fabric of its motions. They have thought that they wrote in order to communicate, and have celebrated their own communion with the old forms, or with the idea that they were making new ones.

Some have written in order to be well-off, a double

idolatry, and others in order to be well-known, a double irony turned in upon itself, and without humor.

So many have written only to be or only to appear, well-versed, and sadly have succeeded in doing only that.

Many write in order to hold on to the past, and many to forget it. A few write in order to create the present and fewer still are sufficiently in the present to create a future within it, and from it.

Maybe it's about time some of us did nothing for the fun of it.

What I am thinking about is observations. I have observed what I have thought, felt, experienced. I don't know how it is that I know that you are interested, but I do.

I claim your interest in part by the qualities of this writing. It is such a claim that all writing makes, and we call such a claim, our recognition of such a claim, its authority. Writing is always political.

Writing is seldom polite. It claims an inappropriate authority, or an inappropriate portion of authority, or both.

We have to think about the degree of authority we demand, and the kind of that authority. The abuse of the reader by the writer must stop. The abuse of the writer by the writer is implicit in abusing the reader, and so both must stop.

Make sure that your writing doesn't far outdistance your experience of life, and don't let it fall behind. Don't limit experience to thinking about it.

There's nothing worse to be experiencing than historicism in the making.

Religiosity pales by comparison.

Nothing is easier to ignore, because the manufacture of historicism is the substance of life as we know it. And no one ignores it more easily than the artist, who seldom fails to contribute to it, a pretender to the absolute.

A pretender, of sorts.

The artist contributes best to this unfortunate manufacture. An inordinate respect for the craft, a more inordinate regard for the artist's own ability, combined with a disregard for the substance of the work, and the lives involved in it, make this sickeningly inevitable.

So much happens to thwart expectations that the deliberate fabrication of expectation is inarticulate with stupidity. When articulation is at the service of this misguided task, it dulls even our apprehension.

It is with this as with other things, all other things, perhaps, a question of how to use, or more simply to spend, to pass, one's time, of how to give and of how to take pleasure, in order to enjoy the available satisfactions.

It seems that for some, and perhaps most for those who equally think with words and write with thoughts, it is necessary first to think about it, to take the pleasure in that, and to take it until the feeling of it is equal to the thought. When neither matters more than the other then the truth of the experience might be able to be written.

I don't understand the contagious notion that one writes for a reason. People eat first to live and second for pleasure. But to think like that is absurd, and to express it makes a travesty of the redundancies.

We write for pleasure, which is not a reason. We write with pleasure. The other feelings which accompany writing are superfluous. They may interest us as we write in showing us what we are, what we were or will be, but to the writing they must be nothing at all. Sorry to rub it in.

Things may not be as they should be, but by the time we leave they could be.

I feel like an adult and a man.

Someone will remember that I was once very much the writer of what I wrote. And I notice, with as little affectation as possible, that I am the writer of this.

This then, which has to do with not writing, is written by someone who wrote, assiduously and seriously, and who again writes this. This is then probably other than what might be thought by someone who hasn't written, who doesn't write, and who might well think little or not at all about it.

It's not important to be thinking this, or like this, but it is good for me. You can think about it.

I have never written anything with such disinterest or with such pleasure as that with which I am now writing this. Not even a letter home.

The best thing better than writing without rough effort is good sex. For example. These are the ways we know we're alive, and these are the things we do with it.

It's better if at the beginning you can see the end. It makes things clearer and you can get more of what you want. It's better if you can tell the end from the beginning.

It's not a good idea to get attached to that end, but it's not so good to stay attached to the beginning either. The middle is so good. But of course you can't stay there. You have to see the end.

I don't particularly see why I should bother to connect this with writing.

Using the world without knowing what it means.

That will have been the other side of this piece of text, the incipient, pragmatic side, the side full of feeling. Of course, feeling is everywhere. And to that side, this piece, as we, are entitled.

Writing without feeling, as we have already expostulated, is dreadful. By that feeling we meant equally feeling for and in the world. We did mean that, didn't we?

An assault on the world is pathetic which uses language as its force.

The world is where and what we live, and language is a noise we make usually because we can't help it.

You're distinct people. You might find things even more pleasant if you found things even more distinctly your own to say. That would mean having to find your own self in the world, and using the world for what it already means, and only then for what it already can be made to mean.

When the world uses you it uses you well. When you then use it you use it better than if you had stopped living it in order only or very nearly only to think about, thinking you're thinking it.

I'll thank you for that.

REMARKS ON WITTGENSTEIN'S REMARKS ON FRAZER'S GOLDEN BOUGH

I may read Deleuze while waiting to sell to a customer. A student may participate in a campus or other revolution while completing her MBA. An artist may remake some portion of the culture while benefiting materially from that culture's interest in what he has undone. Actions of these sorts are no longer contradictory. It is no longer the value of things exchanged which motivates the confusions surrounding the various terms and equations of exchange value. We experience increasingly that it is not those terms, those things and actions, which are of value. They are not. It is the experience of exchange value, as such, which is increasingly valued. It is the erotic stuff of our experience. This is what is meant by currency, the ongoing immediate experience of exchanges and participations within and without constraint.

It is remarkable to find Wittgenstein at the beginning of this slight text, which was moreover unintended as such, speaking about truth as though it existed, and bolstering the contention implicit in that word by contrasting it with error. Perhaps nothing in language is as seductive to the person who enjoys thinking in it, as the numerous pairs of apparent opposites. Truth is surely something we will be rid of if we are to get through the world according to language, to the experience of the world. We will have to dissolve these words, and these present words, and have no more need of them.

This was written in response to Ludwig Wittgenstein's *Remarks on Frazer's Golden Bough*, Brynmill/Humanities, 1979.

We must be more than rid of those angst-ridden moments which rid us of our lives. That revolution, alone, is not enough to engender us. We must see the last, also, of those numerous gestalt-laden matrices and transcripts whereby we all too often live our lives some moments late.

We do not learn from our mistakes; we repeat them. What we may learn is gradually to experience each new moment freshly. In this way we learn always from what we have not completed doing, and thinking and feeling and being and so on. For this reason, truths can only be lies that have happened to other people, ourselves among them.

He is absolutely right when he nonetheless moves on from his own earlier thoughts to note that we need have no use for explanations, and no need of opinions.

> I think one reason why the attempt to find an explanation is wrong is that we have only to put together in the right way what we *know*, without adding anything, and the satisfaction we are trying to get from the explanation comes of itself.
>
> And error belongs only with opinion.

That is how I also would put together what I know. Writing as explanation is dead when we can rather either know what happens or make happen what we know. And writing as an aid to memory is a metaphor for what we would forget.

Gertrude Stein — "If you are explaining, the same thing is true, because if it is a whole thing it does not need explaining, it merely needs stating."

From at least one point of view it is possible, and perhaps even necessary, to view all of the history of human life on this planet, all of the people and actions and thoughts and so on of which we would usually think of it as being composed, as a single event. This point of view, which anyone might take, we might imagine to be necessary to a being wishing to compare the scope of human life to the present with, say, the scope of a race of beings as they might exist, for example, among the Pleiades. From this point of view it would be unnecessary or, as we have imagined it, even impossible, to question an action, asking of it, is this a political action, a reflex one, a ritualistic one, an emotional one, a meaningful one, and so on. It could be unnecessary to question an action.

Wittgenstein registers an important distrust of inferences and synopses, particularly those of an historical nature, by which events which might merely have been described, are instead assumed the one to have generated the other, or which are then summarized as if that were how time worked, and were not merely one of the ways in which its description might be extrapolated. Such extrapolation or extension, and this is my argument, is done for profit; a simple fact, or even a description, a broad fact, is worthless. Against this extrusion of details, he posits as a positive what he describes as "übersichtlich," and which is translated as "perspicuous" as in "a perspicuous presentation." If this were to be taken as a proscription, and were to be followed as one, it would mean that we would describe or state things clearly and in an organized manner, with a view perhaps to easy understanding by another. It would leave to auditor or reader the productions of meanings, insofar as we have understood meaning in the Western manner, to mean *something*. Western language and discourse could be characterized by the transitive verb, and so could most of our behavior.

On the other hand, we may wish to say to someone who makes only a simple observation, such as "It's raining." or even "It was raining." — "May your observations be reproduced in triplicate."

It remains remarkable that we wish to ask in relation to things, are they the same or are they different. This is similar to the crisis of the formulation, "my body," as if these two words could in any way be separated. It might be assumed that this notion, this experience, of separation, arises from the fact that we designate "different" things, concepts, etc., by "different" words. But it does not. It is our experience of the joining together of words, of concepts, etc., which gradually comes to fix in our minds the sense or the notion of their separateness.

Odd, isn't it?

Wittgenstein — "The most noticeable thing seems to me not merely the similarities but also the differences throughout all these rites." The most important word in this statement is "me" because it is that word that is entirely opened by its allegiance at once to similarities and to differences. How much simpler (and we might wish to pose that as a question) is a statement such as this — "In all these practices we see something that is similar, at any rate, to the association of ideas and related to it." — which, at any rate, betrays its allegiance to the quandary of sameness and difference, by a connection with only one of its terms.

One of philosophy's most naked problems is its unwillingness or inability to see with its eyes. Wittgenstein involves himself in an effort to understand why we say of an experience or of a practice that it is deep, or sinister. On the surface he is dealing with the nature of the mystical or the religious. But beneath that, and almost certainly unintentionally, the broader question being asked is: Why do we adjectivize at all? How do we come to say that of that? It is in the context of this that he asks, "But could I not just as well ask: When I see someone killed — is it simply what I see that makes an impression on me, or does this come with the hypothesis that someone is being killed here?" You can see that I leave him with credit for his double interrogative, but I can't help but wonder what it is that makes him experience a difference between what he sees and what he thinks he sees.

CRITICAL ARTICLES CHRONOLOGICALLY

notes for CONSTRUCTION
> (unpublished)

MODES

> TEMBLOR, Issue Number 5, 1987, ed. Leland
?s to .s Hickman
> THE DIFFICULTIES, Vol. 2, No. 2, 1985, ed.
> Tom Beckett

U N A D O R N E D ca78
> (unpublished)

U N A T T R I B U T E D ca 79
> a fragment published in L=A=N=G=U=A=G=E,
> Vol. 2 Nos. 3 and 4, October 1979, ed. Bruce
> Andrews & Charles Bernstein
> a fragment reprinted in The L=A=N=G=U=A=G=E
> Book, Southern Illinois University Press, 1984, ed.
> Bruce Andrews and Charles Bernstein

PLANISHING HAMMER
> L=A=N=G=U=A=G=E, Vol. 2 No. 2, June 1979,
> ed. Bruce Andrews & Charles Bernstein

CENTURY   ARTICLE   80
> (unpublished)

This predilection for the mind in art. Where did I get it?
> L=A=N=G=U=A=G=E, Vol. 3 No. 1, January
> 1980, ed. Bruce Andrews & Charles Bernstein
> reprinted in Poets at the Public LANGUAGE/
> NOISE flier, January 11, 1982

reprinted in PUBLIC LANGUAGE, WIDEMOUTH
#8616 (cassette), 1982, ed. Michael Tolson
reprinted in The L=A=N=G=U=A=G=E Book,
Southern Illinois University Press, 1984, ed.
Bruce Andrews and Charles Bernstein

Private Enigma in the Opened Text
L=A=N=G=U=A=G=E, Vol. 3 No. 3, December
1980, ed. Bruce Andrews & Charles Bernstein
reprinted in The L=A=N=G=U=A=G=E Book,
Southern Illinois University Press, 1984, ed. Bruce
Andrews and Charles Bernstein

If topology were the place the word came from,
THE DIFFICULTIES, I, 1, 1980, ed. Tom Beckett
& Earel Neikirk

ESSAI A CLEF
L=A=N=G=U=A=G=E, Vol. 3 No. 2, June 1980,
ed. Bruce Andrews & Charles Bernstein

The Indeterminate Interval: From History to Blur
(in collaboration with Nick Piombino)
L=A=N=G=U=A=G=E, vol. 4, 1981, ed. Bruce
Andrews & Charles Bernstein

Speech is relatively durable, language a dry solid waste.
THE DIFFICULTIES, Volume 1, 2, Winter 1980 -
1981, ed. Tom Beckett

ABUTTAL
originally presented as a talk at Sally Silvers' loft,
NYC, on April 2, 1981
Casement Books, 1982, published by Michael
Gottlieb

SKIN
originally presented as a talk at Collective for
Living Cinema, NYC, on April 20, 1982 in the
IMAGE/TALK series coordinated by Abigail Child

PURSUE VERITABLE SIMPLES
PURSUE VERITABLE SIMPLES/SEND US THE
DIFFICULT JOBS, Annex Supplement No. 1,

1983, published by Tod Kabza

LIES

THE PARIS REVIEW, 86, 1982, Language Sampler, ed. Charles Bernstein

CLOSE READING CLOSE READING

POETICS JOURNAL, Number 2, September 1982, ed. Lyn Hejinian and Barrett Watten

LANGUAGE
MIND
WRITING

originally presented as a talk at 80 Langton Street, San Francisco, on October 29, 1982 in a series coordinated by Barrett Watten

excerpted and with audience conversation included, in WRITING/TALKS, Southern Illinois University Press, 1985, ed. Bob Perelman

IF WORDS HAD MEANING

originally presented as a talk at Segue, NYC, on March 27, 1984 in the New York Talk series coordinated by Charles Bernstein

"43 Poets (1984)" in BOUNDARY 2, Volume XIV, Number 1, 2, Fall 1985/Winter 1986, ed. Charles Bernstein

Remarks on Wittgenstein's Remarks on Frazer's Golden Bough, TEMBLOR, Issue Number 3, 1986, ed. Leland Hickman

ZEN? WHO KNOWS?

GALLERY WORKS SEVEN, 1987, ed. Peter Holland and Jeanne Lance